What If?

What If?

✦

Contemplations of an Undergrad

Christy Clarke

iUniverse, Inc.
New York Bloomington Shanghai

What If?
Contemplations of an Undergrad

iUniverse books may be ordered through booksellers or by contacting:

iUniverse
1663 Liberty Drive
Bloomington, IN 47403
www.iuniverse.com
1-800-Authors (1-800-288-4677)

Because of the dynamic nature of the Internet, any Web addresses
or links contained in this book may have changed
since publication and may no longer be valid.

ISBN: 978-0-595-44353-6 (pbk)
ISBN: 978-0-595-88682-1 (ebk)

Printed in the United States of America

To my mom, you have taught me so much and your support means everything to me. And to KC, for your constant inspiration and living symbolism of my greatest dreams.

Contents

Introduction

This book is a compilation of thoughts and essays written in my first three Undergrad years at St. Thomas University. In these years I have come to contemplate some different things about my beliefs and the world I live in, and that is what is reflected in the pages that follow, beginning with an exploration of the relationship between science and religion.

When considering this issue, I was compelled to offer a description of my personal ontology. This set of beliefs is what I hold as true. I can't really say I arrived at this set of beliefs or that I developed them, but rather they revealed themselves to me one night, like a memory unfolding while I was talking on the phone with my boyfriend (at the time). I am excited to have written down how I feel and what I believe in this book because of so many similar beliefs and theories I have heard recently from one lecturer, book or another and especially since the release of *The Secret*. It is wonderful to know that not only do others believe similar theories as mine, but that they are being released and welcomed into the world as well.

In recent months, more and more frequently I have been exposed to some piece of information that fits perfectly with this revelation I had just a few years ago. They all seem to be bits of a greater picture and certainly all flow in the same theme. I have come to find myself surrounded with clues and information about several different forms of natural or alternative healing traditions and therapies to the point that last summer, just about every new person I met or old friend I reconnected with led to a conversation about this very subject. So I finally took the hint and began studying more deeply into this field, and life has continued to be more rewarding since then. More and more information and people have come into my life and contributed something to my learning and/or offered a platform for me to share with them a bit of my own experiences and accumulation of knowledge. Ultimately it has lead me to realize that paying attention and responding to life's 'coincidences' is an incredibly powerful and exhilarating method of proceeding with one's life. There are unbelievable messages to be received and lessons to be learned with this practice, and as those of you familiar with the teaching of *The Secret*, it really all boils down to gratitude for everything, and the ability to focus that gratitude on the present.

As I allowed myself to recognize all of those 'coincidences' that summer and decided I had best respond before the Universe hit me upside the head with these hints, I started seriously studying two different forms of energy or vibrational healing therapies which I explain in this book. Studying this has led me to meet some wonderful people and helped me learn more about myself as well as inspired a more clear crystallization of my ultimate life goals and dreams. I want to open a ranch, dedicated to healing both people and animals. I want it to be a rescue and rehabilitation center and adoption program for animals, particularly horses (as you will probably recognize in the pages to follow, I am and have been for as long as I can remember, infected with an equine obsession to which my family can attest). But I want my ranch to be a relaxing and rejuvenating place for people suffering as well. Most importantly, I envision this place to help all sorts of beings heal physical ailments, but the focus will predominantly be on emotional healing, truly deep, whole healing. It is a beautiful place and operation, and I have actually drawn out exactly what the layout of the hundreds of acres it will require will look like, all I'm waiting for now is the financial backing to make it happen–but I believe that is on its way as well.

It was because of an event, or perhaps it would be better described as a process, during my preliminary study of vibrational healing that inspired the idea of writing a book. Then once I wrote out what will form the first section of this book in a paper for school, I realized *that* was what I wanted to publish. So, from that starting point I began reflecting on what else I have written that I would like to share with the world, or anyone interested in reading the written form of my contemplations, and compiled the rest of the contents of this book from there, based on my passions (namely horses, healing, and respect).

In any case, this is a little insight into me, Christy Clarke, and the reasoning behind this book. It is not meant to flow like a novel. Nor is it meant to really form a continuous argument, though the principal theme is the connectivity between everything in the universe, leading to a respect for all life and the reality of "vibrational healing." While this may still seem odd for a book, I wanted it to be precisely what its pieces are: relatively separate and distinctive thoughts, contemplations, and beliefs, connected in the sense that they stem from the same heart and passion, but unique and somewhat disjointed as thoughts and contemplations manifest. I think of this book as a bit of an enhanced diary, sharing with those who turn its pages some of my deepest and strongest beliefs and passions. It is a bit more refined than a diary, and significantly greater contemplation and research has gone into each piece than one would expect to find in a typical diary entry. However, the contents are potentially controversial to some, and I do not expect that anyone will necessarily agree one hundred percent with everything I have written–it is mine; my thoughts, my beliefs. It's okay for them to remain that way. But I felt compelled to write them once upon a time (within the past three years) and then more recently felt compelled to compile and publish them independently. This book is the product of my exploration of myself, my world and a response to all those 'coincidences' and compulsions leading me to put it into print.

If you choose to read this book I thank you for being open to the idea of reading someone's thoughts and beliefs, knowing that you may disagree entirely with what I have written and that the fortunate or unfortunate (depending on your perspective) thing about a book is, it is a one-sided conversation. I hope that I have articulated myself clearly in each of these essays, and I hope you enjoy my thoughts.

What If?

The debate between science and religion is an incredibly complex one. There is no simple solution because there are many religions and religious sub sects and also there are many different branches and views of science. We need to compare them all in order to arrive at a concrete solution. Both are theoretical social structures claiming to hold and/or search for absolute 'truth' but there are very significant differences between them. Science is an academic field with practical applications, tests, and models of the world and universe in which we exist. It studies everything from the smallest particles to the systems and bodies in outer space and everything in between, but its studies are limited to tangible elements. Science does not study belief sets or values. In fact, it claims to be 'value-neutral' or 'value-free,' but most critics have arrived at the conclusion that it does indeed embody values; it embodies the values of the general Western culture, which makes their presence more difficult to identify in practice.

Karl Barth, a twentieth century Christian theologian and neo-orthodox thinker is known to have held the view that science and religion are two different and complementary things. He would argue that theology is one kind of thing and science is another, so there is no conflict. Science is the study of things, and would for example describe the size and shape of an object while theology or religion will describe the colour and design of the same object—both are correct, but they are different kinds of descriptions of what is; they are complementary descriptions that explore different properties of the same thing and thus do not conflict. For Barth, science is just people exploring their natural environment but it doesn't tell us anything about God.[1]

This may be true to a degree, because science is missing an element of religion—that is faith: belief, without proof, in any number of things. Likewise religion lacks an element of science—the need for comprehendible, physiological explanations of everything. They may well both search for the 'truth' and they

---

1. Richard Dickinson, <u>Karl Barth</u>, and Thomas Aquinas, "How Do We Know God? (A Radio Conversation between Karl Barth and Thomas Aquinas)" *Journal of Bible and Religion*, Vol. 26, No. 1 (Jan., 1958): 38-43.

may both be human constructions, but one is an intellectual, practical study of the universe and the other is more of an emotional, theoretical belief of humility in our existence alongside something much greater, be it God, Earth or the universe, or many gods. From this perspective it seems the two *should* be able to coexist peacefully without problem. However, there is much evidence that this is simply not the case.

Since religion as a practice typically offers people a set of guidelines by which to live their life, and a belief set that includes an idea of what is right and wrong, good and bad, its very essence is *about* constructing, promoting and facilitating values. In its own effort to maintain objectivity, science often takes being 'value-free' to mean in practice it must be free from restrictions of values or certain belief sets. This then leads to scientific practice that *conflicts* with many religious values–by not having values construct guidelines or boundaries to scientific practice there is room for experiments that would otherwise be unethical or immoral. When science, for example, claims to be value-free and objective, but performs traumatic and/or painful or lethal experiments on non-human animals and this is offensive to others it cannot very well maintain its value-free claim. If it were truly value-free there would be no conflicts with its practices, but when something done in the name of science contests or provokes someone's belief or value set, it is actually doing work that employs the *opposite* values as those perturbed by the work. This fact makes it easier for us to locate unconscious values *in* science. Anywhere someone's personal or religious values conflict or are offended, there is evidence of values embodied in *that* science.

Another problem between science and religion comes when scientific discoveries contradict or disprove what is written in sacred texts or is held as true by religious groups. Creation stories are a huge factor in this element of the science vs. religion debate, as they are often contradicted by modern science's cosmological theory–the 'big bang'. The 'big bang' is supposed to have happened billions of years ago, and have taken millions more to evolve to this point at present. Most creation stories include one or more gods existing and deciding to, or accidentally 'creating' the universe and everything in it in a matter of a few days. This is true of the Christian story, the Islamic story, Australia's Aboriginal peoples' story, and many Native American stories of creation. The idea of creation may have less difficulty with scientific theory if it were not so often described as taking place in such a short period of time, for this seems to be the main conflict; science does not offer an explanation for what happened before or even 'why' the 'big bang' occurred, for which the idea of creation may well complement. However, when the creation stories suggest everything that has come to exist as we know it today was what came to be during creation, and it all arose in a matter of days, typically, scientific theory conflicts. The latter suggests that everything started instead from particles colliding in space and gaining stronger and stronger force as more and more particles were attracted to the original molecule. Over time, lots of time—billions of years even—the universe as we know it came to be. After copious evolution, things have all originated from single celled organisms and eventually we have arrived with the diversity we know today.

For those who take their creation stories literally this is problematic, because science which was supposed to be value-free is in fact heretical to their own beliefs and values. They are posed with a choice, either to accept this new science and update or abandon their religion, or to negate or refuse to accept the scientific claims—after all, according to sociologists they too may just be man-made stories that a group of people agree to agree are true, without actual empirical and indisputable 'proof'. The purposes sacred stories and texts serve are not dissimilar to many of the culturally developed stories we are exposed to as children. Both of these have morals and or lessons to teach the person listening something important about how to act appropriately or what to believe to be true. Both cultural and sacred stories often involve extraordinary or fantastical characters in unordinary situations to exaggerate the point. I believe this is because both these types of stories are intended to teach, and often when something is being taught, the learner is inexperienced and such exaggerations make them more easily understandable for anyone in the early stages of learning any discipline, concept, tradition, or belief. This may provide explanation for why animals are often used in such stories and given human qualities and characteristics such as the ability to speak. Both these types of stories are designed to make sense of confusing rules and structures of either cultural or religious societies.

One thing about these types of stories is that they are just that, stories. They were told first by a person, then passed on through oral tradition and eventually written down. That means essentially that they were created by people, and can just as easily be destroyed by people. *Religion, A Search for Meaning* by Margaret C Huff and Ann K Wetherilt, describes how parts of the Christian Bible differ from sect to sect, and whole parts are actually left out in some cases.[2] This makes it difficult to determine how much truth one can justify attributing to any particular sacred story or text. The issue of translation is raised on those same pages, and addresses the issue of not only difficulty surpassing language barriers when

---

2.   Margaret C. Huff & Ann K. Wetherilt, *Religion: A Search For Meaning*. (New York: McGraw-Hill, 2005), 212-220.

translating these sacred stories and texts, but perhaps a much more difficult barrier of translating such works to make sense in very different time periods. Few scholars would argue it can be difficult to understand even Shakespeare's work, (not written very long ago, considering the time-span of human existence) even if English is their first language. That outlines a huge problem when sacred stories and texts from over one thousand years ago, or more in some cases, are necessarily translated from sometimes extinct languages to modern times and dialects.

I would like to look briefly at a few examples of creation stories, and then offer a description of my own set of beliefs, my personal spiritual philosophies as an alternative to organized religion altogether. My beliefs are just that, mine and I expect they will only ever be held as completely true by me, but they, unlike most if not all religions do not conflict with modern science and subsequently offer an alternative perspective to the entire debate. My philosophies are based on the structure of the atom, it complements the 'big bang' theory, but the rest of the concepts remain outside the field of scientific study—to my knowledge. They are ideas about what life *is*, and how we 'fit' into the universe in relation to everything else on a spiritual level. If science truly *was* value-free, it would not contest any element of my philosophies at all. But first, let's look at some more widely known and accepted creation stories.

Many indigenous peoples' creation stories do involve a creator, or God, or several gods who are often animals. Their stories often include god-animals with human qualities such as the ability to speak, and subsequently respect the creatures of the Earth with spiritual reverence, viewing them as keepers of spiritual guidance and wisdom instead of resources to be dominated and exploited.

The Australian Aboriginal creation stories often place animals in major roles. It is interesting to consider the characteristics, emotions and levels of intelligence these historical stories often place on non-human animals when they are taught to children. It is no wonder children's innate fascination with nature is further developed as they learn the stories of their culture that seem to always have animal heroes and heroines. It seems slightly hypocritical then, to consider the common (at least the North American) adult perception that animals are inferior to humans and have little to no intelligence outside instinct, needing to be disrespected. Is it not strange how that changes so drastically?

The Karraur Tribe of Australia's creation story goes as follows:

> Once the earth was completely dark and silent; nothing moved on its barren surface. Inside a deep cave below the Nullabor Plain slept a beautiful woman, the Sun. The Great Father Spirit gently woke her and told her to emerge from

her cave and stir the universe into life. The Sun mother opened her eyes and darkness disappeared as her rays spread over the land; she took a breath and the atmosphere changed; the air gently vibrated as a small breeze blew.

The Sun Mother then went on a long journey; from north to south and from east to west she crossed the barren land. The earth held the seed potencies of all things, and wherever the Sun's gentle rays touched the earth, there grasses, shrubs, and trees grew until the land was covered in vegetation. In each of the deep caverns in the earth, the Sun found living creatures which, like herself, had been slumbering for untold ages. She stirred the insects into life in all their forms and told them to spread through the grasses and trees, then she woke the snakes, lizards, and other reptiles, and they slithered out of their deep hole. As the snakes moved through and along the earth they formed rivers and they themselves became creators, like the Sun. Behind the snakes mighty rivers flowed, teeming with all kinds of fish and water life. Then she called for the animals, the marsupials, and the many other creatures to awake and make their homes on the earth. The Sun Mother then told all the creatures that the days would from time to time change from wet to dry and from cold to hot, and so she made the seasons. One day while all the animals, insects, and other creatures were watching, the Sun traveled far in the sky to the west and, as the sky shone red, she sank from view and darkness spread across the land once more. The creatures were alarmed and huddled together in fear. Some time later, the sky began to glow on the horizon to the east and the Sun rose smiling in the sky again. The Sun Mother thus provided a period of rest for all her creatures by making this journey each day.[3]

The Christian creation story is a little different. It is written in the book of Genesis in the Old Testament of the Bible. To summarize the story, God created Heaven and Earth, speaking everything into existence. He would say, 'let there be light' and it would appear. He first created and established a difference between light and darkness and subsequently formed morning and night, and our concept of time in 'days'. Over a period of six days he created everything else, the earth, the sky, and the water. Then he created plants and animals and eventually humans. As the story goes God created only two humans at first, a man and then a woman. The man He made from the earth, the clay, and then the woman God made from a rib of the man to be his partner. To the humans, God granted

---

3.   Margaret C. Huff & Ann K. Wetherilt, *Religion: A Search For Meaning*, (New York: McGraw-Hill, 2005), 191; excerpt from Robert Lawlor, *Voices of the First Day: Awakening the Aboriginal Dreamtime* (Rochester, VT: Inner Traditions International, 1991), 88.

dominion over everything. He made them in His image and so they were special. This is the basic Christian story of creation.

The Islamic creation story is very similar in appearance to the Christian one. Allah, the Muslim God, is said to have also created the universe in six days, commanding or again speaking it into existence. There is a difference though, in the meaning of 'days'. In the Qur'an the same Arabic term for 'day' is used to describe different periods of time.

> The verses that mention "six days" use the Arabic word "youm" (day). This word appears several other times in the Qur'an, each denoting a different measurement of time. In one case, the measure of a day is equated with 50,000 years (70:4), whereas another verse states that "a day in the sight of your Lord is like 1,000 years of your reckoning" (22:47). The word "youm" is thus understood, within the Qur'an, to be a long period of time—an era or eon. Therefore, Muslims interpret the description of a "six day" creation as six distinct periods or eons.[4]

This allows the Islamic creation story significantly more congruence and less conflict with modern science and the 'big bang' theory.

For me, the beginning just was. It corresponds with modern cosmology's 'big bang' theory that at some point particles came together and then continued to gather. In science, even the smallest particles–electrons and protons, or even smaller still, quarks–all have an energetic charge. This is true also of my personal views–there is constant and continuous energy in everything, absolutely everything. 'Stuff' or bodies are the physical manifestation of collective masses of this energy, but it exists on another level, for me, in a non-physical realm–one we can't see, but that exists where we think; the 'mental stuff' or the 'soul'. My views can accept the 'big bang' theory in its entirety; all those many years of evolution are perfectly consistent with my belief that energy just *is* and continues to *be* and change form through time, and it can be progressive. Further, my views of what came before the 'beginning' are simply that the energy was in a different form but has always existed, infinitely back in 'time'.

For me, the concept of 'time' is also a human construct, as with other forms of measurement–it is relative and representative of *us* and functional for how *we* perceive the world and universe. The scales are suited for our understanding, but are insignificant in the larger scope of existence. For me the more important

---

4.   About.com, "Creation of the Universe". (2006 About, Inc: The New York Times Company), http://islam.about.com/od/creation/a/creation.htm

'stuff' is emotional, intellectual, cognitive functions of interaction with, and respect for, but not necessarily understanding *of* our world and everything in it. For me it is irrelevant how big or small, physically similar or different things are, but what their relationship to me and everything else in the universe is, is reflective of what 'matters' in life, according to my philosophies. That said, when we think of what came before the 'beginning' it seems irrational to think of it in terms of a speed or length of time as we know it to exist on our planet, considering at that point our planet did not exist. To apply a construct of human rationality to something prior to our own existence, or at least the existence of the environment necessary for our existence, is simply inappropriate–in my opinion. Who is to say there was a 'before' at all?

While it seems impractical to understand the beginnings of the universe without applying human concepts that in turn facilitate human logic and comprehension, it also seems impossible to impose such concepts on things and events so much greater than ourselves which occurred in our absence. To impose these human constructs implies that it is simple enough for us to understand, or that we are sophisticated and intelligent enough to do so, but why? It seems to me such things are beyond our cognitive capacity, it would be arrogant and naïve to assume it might even be possible for us to conceptualize life beyond that which we experience ourselves. We have a difficult enough time attempting to understand how other species on our own planet experience the world and life in general. How can we possibly expect to understand life outside a universe we know— that is, the current state of our universe? For me, accepting humility is essential to living, experiencing, and coming to recognize our life's purpose.

Religion itself is a complex subject. Everyone believes in something, but not everyone believes in a well-established and clearly defined religion, or any religion at all, for that matter. Some people believe in their religion because it was what they were taught their whole life, others have been influenced by people or writings or events in their lives that have lead them to come to accept a set of religious beliefs as defined by one religious organization or another. Some people have changed their religious beliefs over the course of their life, in response to experiences or ideas that conflicted with their prior beliefs. It seems for most people they can define themselves in some way, by religion–either they believe in one or they do not. But then, there are many people who just don't know where they fit in their belief structure, and others whose attitudes, values and beliefs tend to remain unfixed for periods of time and shift to correlate with continuous life events.

Certainly there is no shortage of 'options' for one seeking a title of religious organization to categorize themselves under, with so many distinctly different organizations and many of them with dozens of their own sub-sects. Still there are many people who simply cannot classify themselves as 'fitting' with any of these options. This is not to suggest that our belief sets and values are things we acquire simply by picking and choosing, they are deep rooted feelings that are what we hold as guidelines for what is right and wrong and how to live our life in order to be good people. But for some people, their belief sets simply do not fit with the predetermined ones outlined by traditional and/or organized religions. I happen to be one of those people. One of the primary factors of why I don't feel like I 'fit' in any one organized religious group is because I do not want to have my beliefs or values defined by anything or anyone other than myself. I feel that defining oneself by a traditional religious group has many limitations, restrictions, and sometimes unwanted or inaccurate connotations. If I said to someone, "I am a Christian" that might mean I am a caring, giving, honest and good person while to someone else who has had a traumatic experience with another person who defined themselves as a Christian, the term then means something completely different. When we begin defining ourselves with such broad titles we inadvertently invite others to make assumptions about what those titles mean, but this can be problematic when such titles are used by many people in different contexts. When there are many sects within a religion for example, with Christianity one may call themselves Christian but not follow the Catholic traditions and in fact locate themselves under another title under the alternate sub-sects of Protestantism.

In a recent radio interview I was sternly asked by the host, who did not consider himself a Christian, to defend Christianity. I told him that I couldn't do it, and moreover, that I didn't want to defend the term. He asked me if I was a Christian, and I told him yes. "Then why don't you want to defend Christianity?" he asked, confused. I told him I no longer knew what the term meant. Of the hundreds of thousands of people listening to his show that day, some of them had terrible experiences with Christianity; they may have been yelled at by a teacher in a Christian school, abused by a minister, or browbeaten by a Christian parent. To them, the term *Christianity* meant something that no Christian I know would defend. By fortifying the term, I am only making them more and more angry. I won't do it. Stop ten people on the street and ask them what they think of when they hear the word *Christianity*, and they will give you ten different answers. How can I defend a term that means ten different things to ten different people? I told the radio show host that I would rather talk about Jesus and how I came to believe that Jesus exists and that He likes me.[5]

I think this is an excellent illustration. Organized religion itself and terminology people construct can gain such horrible reputations, which make it difficult for anyone to confidently identify themselves with a religious title that may mean something different to, as the quote says–ten different people. Yet, describing and defending the beliefs and spiritual passions that we feel naturally compelled to hold as true is so much more accurate a description of what it means to be spiritual, and to be a living example of just that. People have created a significant difference between what it means to be religious and what it means to be spiritual, the more we stop defending titles the closer we will come to defining real truth.

Titles always carry with them meanings, and religious titles are no different. The problem arises when we define ourselves with broad titles, like 'Christian' or 'Buddhist' or 'Muslim' for example, which also have multiple sub-sects. With such definitions of ourselves we do invite others to make assumptions about our beliefs, values and traditions based on what their understanding of that title means. This is also not to say that to make such assumptions is right or just, but it occurs nonetheless and as a consequence we have multiple representations of single broad titles created as different individuals or groups advertise these titles in correlation to different acts or practices. This is where confusion begins and religious stereotyping is born–when acts or practices are done or justified in the name of some broad religious title, or people define who they are and how they behave by their religious beliefs, which may or my not match those of the majority of the other members of such a religion. We see this happening today with the Islam faith.

While about one quarter of the world's population today defines themselves as Islamic, the common Western idea of what a Muslim is, is a Middle Eastern Arab terrorist, who believes in suicide bombing and fighting the non-Islamic world. But, considering there are more Nigerians and Indonesians who are Muslim than all of those who live in the Middle East, this perception is significantly inaccurate. In fact, to believe that all Muslims are terrorists is just outright false. This is a perfect example of why it is dangerous to hold such broad titles over belief systems, or to hold titles over belief systems at all. Anyone can claim to be acting based on their beliefs or personal religious values and if they claim to be associated with an organized or titled religion, then they connect themselves to all others who use

5.   Donald Miller, *Blue Like Jazz*, (Nelson Books: 2003), 115.

the same title even though their beliefs and values may differ. This is the problem associated with naming or titling or classification systems in general–they are by their very nature rigid in definition and reductionistic. Titles make it difficult for 'fence sitters' to classify themselves with any group, it just seems awkward to suggest you are, "half Christian, half Muslim" or some other combination–just which half are you then, and what parts constitute the 'half' you pick and choose to accept? Of course, some religions lend themselves to blending, like Soto Zen Buddhism which has no metaphysics and therefore can be easily coupled with a religion like Christianity that does have a structured belief system on metaphysical beings, but has no 'rules' against seated meditation. Such neat 'religious combos' are few and far between though.

So, if one doesn't 'fit' in any organized religion, what do they do? Some call themselves atheists–and do not believe in the existence of a God at all. Others consider themselves agnostic–"somebody who doubts that a particular question has a single correct answer or that a complete understanding of something can be attained."[6] Or, what I would like to propose is the option that one may simply commit to not define themselves by organized religion, and perhaps claim not to be 'religious' at all, but 'spiritual' instead. This statement removes one from having a predetermined title to offer as a description of themselves, frees them from having to accept someone else's definition of their beliefs, and sets them up to offer an exact explanation of their personal values and belief sets that they hold as true. The term 'spiritual' can also be used as a title, but it does not carry the same ideologies as 'religion' and is subsequently less self explanatory thus inviting discussion participants to investigate the meaning of the term as defined by *that* person or context. Spirituality offers a platform to present your belief sets and values that are specific to you. This is something completely different to an organized and finite or concrete religious doctrine that is a predetermined package of values and beliefs. On that note, I would like to offer my personal thoughts on 'creation' and define my own beliefs and values.

Having grown up in a Christian home, in a Christian society it is likely that these views are influenced by Christianity, but at the same time, it was this very society and experiences with multiple 'Christians' that initially lead me to think about my spirituality as something different and separate from the Christian faith. Having witnessed first hand the multiple personalities of this particular organized religion and the intense confusion that can evoke in someone trying to learn about and understand the tradition, it inspired me to recognize those con-

---

6.   Microsoft Office Word Dictionary, 2003.

structed boundaries and limitations of beliefs and determine a greater freedom exists outside of them. It seems my set of beliefs and values came to reveal themselves to me while I was playing a game of "what if" with my boyfriend about how and why life exists, so I'll call what I'm about to describe the "What if" philosophy.

It seems fitting to start at the beginning, so let's start with the idea of creation. It has always seemed perplexing to me that there be one human-like God who created the world and the universe. Who then created that God, how did He, or She, come to exist? Why do some religions have one God and others have multiple gods; and others still, have none at all? And how could a universe come to exist without at least one God? So I began to play my 'what if' game and stumbled upon the question, "what if the universe was created, but there is no creator at all?" There is a certain Buddhist feel to this, but the meaning behind these thoughts is different for me. I distilled that idea down to "what if, God *is* the universe?" This particular 'what if' seemed to inspire in my mind an explosion of questions and ideas that followed suit; what if 'God' did not leave evidence, traces or clues about himself in nature for 'believers' to come to find and see as evidence for his existence, what if instead nature *is* God? What if the images or 'signatures' we see, the 'evidence of design' that makes up natural theology are actually pieces *of* God, not just reflections of His work? What if God does not have a human-like form, or one that resembles any one thing here on Earth, but *is* everything on Earth at the same time? What if humans were not made in God's image, but *everything* was made in God's image, and what if everything *is*, in part, God?

I am aware that all or most of these questions have reflections of some of the most well known religious organizations in them, and I welcome those similarities. I do not deny that pieces of perhaps every organized, titled religion fit into my personal belief set, in fact that is probably the most accurate way for me to describe my views: that they are inter-religious, or they are a mix or blend of all the pieces of each religion I have come to believe as true. No one set of 'organized' religious beliefs seems to fit precisely with what I feel compelled to hold as true, but many parts contribute to the whole that is mine.

I would like to describe what the outcome of all of these 'what ifs' have come to look like in my head, how they manifested into a set of beliefs and values that I currently hold as true to me. It is all based on the idea that there is something greater than myself, a force or power that exists both beyond and within me. I will call that force God for simplicity sake to make this description more coherent, but it is not a God like the Christian God or the Muslim Allah. It is a God with a more Buddhist or Native American flavor—it does not have a human form, it is not male or female, masculine or feminine, it just *is*. My God is not separate from the Earth, but it is not confined to it either. To me, God *is* the universe, and everything in it *is* God.

Once this view had crystallized in my mind, I got a sort of image, a physical idea of what exactly this would look like, and how it could work–realistically–though I do not think that is necessary for a spiritual idea. In order to fully explain this image, we must first look at a bit of science, in particular–the atom. So what are atoms?

According to MNS Encarta, atoms are the particles that make up all matter in the universe. They are the fundamental structures which are used to build literally everything from individual grains of sand, to human beings, to a whole planet. The different elements of the earth which are listed in the chemical periodic table are all different variations of atoms; they all share the same basic structure, with different numbers of protons and electrons. It is through various and complex combinations of these single atoms that eventually form matter.

But what *is* an atom, and why do I include reference to it for my personal spiritual philosophy? Well, the atom represents the tiniest level of my theory–it is the basic structure that makes up all matter greater than it, and in 'its image'–in my opinion. Atoms are electrically charged particles too–they share that distinctive and connected paradoxical energy I believe is what constitutes life. But it is not a simple energy they have–atoms are made up of particle themselves; three different main types: electrons, protons and neutrons, which can then be broken down into smaller particles still–called quarks, of which there is variety too.

The core of the atom is made up of both protons and neutrons in order to be stable. Protons carry a positive charge, and just like magnets would repel each other without the neutrons in place to respond to this. Typically, for every proton an atom has, it also has a matching electron.

> Electrons are tiny, negatively charged particles that form a cloud around the nucleus of an atom … Electrons act differently than everyday objects because electrons can behave as both particles and waves. **Actually, all objects have this property, but the wavelike behavior of larger objects, such as sand, marbles, or even people, is too small to measure.** In very small particles wave behavior is measurable and important. Electrons travel around the nucleus of an atom, but because they behave like waves, they do not follow a specific path like a planet orbiting the Sun does. Instead they form regions of negative electric charge around the nucleus. These regions are called orbitals, and they correspond to the space in which the electron is most likely to be found.[7]

Electrons, however are not located at the core of the atom, they exist in an irregular orbit or cloud outside the core. This basic structure is a mirror image of the greater layers of my theory. Biological systems in earth life forms tend to have regular paths, but may shift from the norm from time to time; humans and non-human life tends to 'orbit' the earth in an irregular pattern, and then so do the water systems on our globe. As far as we know, the larger systems and bodies of the universe tend to travel in more regular 'orbits' but then, our knowledge of these things is limited to what has been tangibly explored or observed by us, which is comparatively minimal.

> Atoms are made of smaller particles, called electrons, protons, and neutrons. An atom consists of a cloud of electrons surrounding a small, dense nucleus of protons and neutrons. Electrons and protons have a property called electric charge, which affects the way they interact with each other and with other electrically charged particles. Electrons carry a negative electric charge, while protons have a positive electric charge. The negative charge is the opposite of the positive charge, and, like the opposite poles of a magnet, these opposite electric charges attract one another. Conversely, like charges (negative and negative, or positive and positive) repel one another. The attraction between an atom's electrons and its protons holds the atom together. Normally, an atom is electrically neutral, which means that the negative charge of its electrons is exactly equaled by the positive charge of its protons.[8]

So, just as my philosophy will explain later, all particles and all beings have an energy and a connection to each other. There are attractive and repulsive forces between us all, and that in balancing these forces we are moving toward harmony as a whole. When things are out of balance in the big, universal picture they are unstable just as with a tiny atom. And just as an atom can break down and change into another one with time, so too do all beings, in my philosophy.

So, what is the relation between how I think of God, the universe and a tiny atom? A very intense one, in fact. To me, the atom is symbolically and literally what both God and the universe look like, just differing in scale, and even so only to a degree. Just as the electrons orbit the nucleus, all of the systems of the universe and our earth seem to orbit some smaller core. It is almost a set of 'nesting' spheres or different layers of systems or things orbiting a smaller core from the

7.   MSN   Encarta.   http://encarta.msn.com/encyclopedia_761567432/Atom.html
      Encyclopedia Article: "Atom". © 2006 Microsoft. (Emphasis added.)
8.   MSN   Encarta.   http://encarta.msn.com/encyclopedia_761567432/Atom.html
      Encyclopedia Article: "Atom". © 2006 Microsoft.

large scale features of the universe to the cells in our body. Reference to a set of 'matryoshki' or Russian stacking dolls, that decrease in size and are poised one inside the other, may be useful imagery here. I will elaborate.

What we know of exactly how the universe works and what exactly it does is incredibly little. The general consensus right now however, is that there are multiple galaxies swirling or orbiting around some point. This is perhaps the largest scale, or level we can go–at least with what current science has to offer. The next level would be the multiple solar systems orbiting within our galaxy. The next level within my matryoshki–like theory would be the planets within our single solar system, each orbiting the Sun. Within that level we can go smaller, to the individual planets, some with single or multiple moons orbiting again. To focus on what we know *most* about we can take this theory to several more levels on planet Earth. First, there are weather and water systems that flow together, the clouds orbiting the globe from a distance, and the liquid water flowing on the surface in lakes, rivers, oceans and tiny streams, as well as all the water systems hidden underground.

Just as the water flows on Earth, so do the living beings. Birds fly all around the globe, some even migrate from pole to pole each year. But in this level non-human animals and humans also exist (a significantly small element in the process, at the same level and equal to other species, not set apart or distinguished in any way from the rest of the system–this is how humans fit in my world view). So, just as the larger levels worked in my theory, humans and animals orbit the Earth in their daily life, in vehicles and by foot. We pulse as a unified group–all mobile creatures on the Earth–from the birds in the sky to ourselves and animals on the earth and the fish in the sea. Tree and plant-life fit into this layer too, while they do not move locations, typically, they are moved by the forces of layers bigger than them–the water and weather. Trees, flowers, grasses, and weeds grow in the sun and rain and dance in the wind. They breathe in as we exhale and vise versa; the next level is similar in all of us unified species as well. For me, the next 'nesting' level are the biological systems within us all–our digestive systems, our circulatory systems, our nervous systems, our respiratory systems–they are all connected, flowing and communicative systems that exist throughout our bodies, necessary for the essential 'stuff' that permits life within us to orbit around our bodies, nourishing us from head to toe and to all the extremities. If we look closer still, open up this level to reveal the one within it, we can keep going. Next we find the cells, the blood cells traveling in the arteries and blood vessels, the neurons that provide us with the senses, the oxygen in our lungs. Finally, we can go even one more step further: within those cells are particles, elements, atoms.

Now, we have looked at our universe from as big as we know it to be and opened it up by layers to reveal different systems working differently, and similarly at the same time, to accomplish both different and similar goals. All of the layers have the same type of structure as the atom, and can eventually be broken down into many of those very building blocks of life. That is the fundamental part of my view, the piece that made it all seem to 'fit' together with my overall ideas. If God *is* the universe, then everything in the universe must also *be* God. This removes humans from a position of superiority, dominion or specialty. We are *all* made of the exact same 'stuff,' we can all be broken down into particles and atoms and ultimately energy. Science has a periodic table of elements that come together in millions of different combinations to form everything from a grain of sand, a drop of rain, a cell of blood, or the universe as a whole. We are all a part of this greater structure that is in essence the same as the tiniest particles that combine to form ourselves. God then, can be found in everything–not just represented in things but actually existing in them. That provides a greater sense of connectedness between all things. This is the physical side of my personal set of beliefs. Next we will consider the component that is what all of these physical things come together to create–life.

This too follows my theme that we are all the same continuous and equal being. To me there isn't a question of what has consciousness and what doesn't– if it is alive, it has a certain energy, because energy is the essence of life. This is what is lost when something dies; its energy changes form, leaves its physical body and takes a different form, perhaps in this place, perhaps in another. The energy that translates, in my view, to the essence of life is one through which all the physical layers, and 'individual' beings of each layer are connected. I would visualize this as a string of smoke that stretches out and swirls in all directions, but is all the same and remains one continuous flow. Each of the 'swirls' may represent one being, growing and changing and ultimately dissipating and flowing back into the original string of smoke.

For me, this is how our lives work. We are born and our energy 'loop' in the ultimate energy 'string' is formed. As we grow and age and experience the world we are moved by the elements in it, and so our 'loop' is shaped, as uniquely contoured as our personalities. Similarly, just as we are influenced by others, we too influence them, and one day we die, and our 'loop' is stretched back out into the core 'string', perhaps to form another 'loop' again in the future. In this sense we are more than just equals, the energy that gives us life is not just the same kind, but is actually all the same, shared energy. This requires removal of hierarchies of sophistication or significance, or dominion. It also removes species boundaries and provides ground for us to be considered equal to the dogs and cats we keep as pets, the trees we grow in our yard, the pigs and cows we eat for dinner, etcetera.

This dismisses the idea that it would be derogatory for one to suggest non-human animal suffering is equivalent to human suffering, and ranks the same on a moral or ethical injustice scale. It also dismisses the idea that to be referred to as a different species or gender is suggestion of insult, that one may be 'reduced' through insult of physiological and/or biological differences. For me, the value of all life is equal, no matter what form it comes in. I believe that all lives have a purpose that was outlined prior to the birth of a soul, or formation of an energy 'loop'. When we follow these 'soul journey's' (to borrow the term from James Redfield in his *Celestine Prophesy* series) we are benefiting and helping the ultimate spiritual growth of the universe as a whole, for then we are traveling the right path, the path that we set out to travel before we even began. When we stray from our soul journeys in my philosophy, we are doing harm to the flow of the universe, no longer existing peacefully and aiding in the overall process or picture, but actually we become parasitic and disruptive to our theoretical layer and in turn, our 'host' earth.

This, I suppose, leads into my views on the 'afterlife'. What fits with my view in terms of an afterlife is a combination of such a dimension existing, and at the same time, not. Since I believe we are all connected points in the same core string of energy, I do not believe that any pieces of the energy die or go away when a life dies on Earth. I simply believe that the energy changes shape, floods out of a 'loop' and into that continuous string again, and the soul travels with it, to another dimension until it identifies another place and path through which it can contribute to the spiritual growth of the universe.

What do I mean by that—the spiritual growth of the universe? Simply that all of these layers of atomically structured, nesting levels of the universe are all moving and working toward one ultimate goal: harmony. When all of the elements, from large scale to the tiniest particles come together in unison, true and ultimate harmony will be reached. But each piece must overcome its Ego, its sense of individual self, and recognize the common goal; each must recognize its insignificance and its opportunity to reach a higher individual state by accepting that it is merely a part of something much bigger than itself, and becoming one with the whole. I heard a joke once that seems in fact a fitting description of just what I mean with this philosophy:

How do you add one plus one, and get one? Well, if you have one pile of bricks and you add it to another pile of bricks, you end up with still one pile of bricks. They may look like separate bricks, but they are made of the same 'stuff' and they come together to form a unified whole–the pile. When we can all embrace humility, to put a human label on it, we will reach what I believe to be the 'point' of the universe, the 'point' of our meager existence in this big expanse that is life.

'Coincidences'–those strangely peculiar and often helpful surprises in life play a big role in my personal belief set. I think they are always much more than that– I think they deliver messages about our soul journeys–either that we are taking the proper steps, the ones we anticipated in our 'soul visions' (to borrow another phrase from Redfield) before life began, or that we are beginning to stray away from it. I think coincidences carry clues about our soul journeys for us to recognize, and it is in how we interpret them that they can provide us with the information necessary for us to embark on our next life 'step'. This process is not so much one of psychic powers, just merely following and trusting our intuition– our connection to the universal energy source and core–but doing so without falling victim to an overactive ego in the process. If we maintain humility and trust that the wisdom we need to succeed in life will come to us when we need it, we will flow through our journey beautifully–this is not to say without struggle, but certainly with a consistent sense of peace and harmony within. When we lose sight of our connection to the greater cause, to the whole, we begin to lose that sense of peace and harmony we enjoyed while benefiting from a connected existence. We also tend to miss the informative and inspirational 'coincidences' that are offered to a harmonious 'us' by the core energy when we are connected.

It is through a respect and appreciation for all life, and unselfish intentions that we gain a true connection with the core energy that we are eternally part of. When such a connection is established we become more sensitive, aware of and attuned to the feeling and purpose of that core energy. We can begin to feel our connection to the other souls in our universal layer, as well as those of the other layers. When this is achieved we can work together using the connected force and power of this humble and unified energy to heal and guide distracted or lost souls back to a recollection of their original soul journey, and the idea of the unified, harmonious whole.

So, what about "fate"? If we have predetermined or pre-planned soul journeys does that mean we are controlled by fate and have no 'free will'? I don't think so. I believe that we do think through a soul journey before we begin the life in order to experience it from beginning to end, but that is just a plan–what we hoped to do and what we hoped to achieve in that life. Most people you ask would tell you they don't recall such a plan, or know where in life they want to be 100 percent of the time. This plan was one set out by our core being, our core energy, that seems to have a faint voice, muffled by the values and opinions we form in response to experiences and influences by other people and things that accumulate as life progresses. That original plan forms our humble and fragile core. It is strongest at birth and early childhood but tends to get lost in our subconscious as we grow and become exposed to the disharmonies in the world when we bury it, tucking it away in our mind to protect it. Most of us tend to have a sense about this plan, even when we forget altogether about its existence. When we accidentally take a step in the right direction we get a split second glimpse of that feeling of harmony, we get excited and inspired that we've made the 'right choice' because we just 'know'—there is a momentary flooding in our bodies and minds of that unified peace as we have awakened our intuition, even if only for a second. Are we governed by the 'fate' of the universe? No. Instead I would argue, from my perspective, that the fate of the universe is governed by the collective choices all of us tiny elements make, whether or not we follow, stray from or return to our soul journey paths.

This then leaves us completely open to the idea of 'free will', in fact it encourages the idea. While there is an outlined life path for us to take, we may or may not follow it. For me, no one's death is 'fated', there are not 'star crossed' lovers, these meetings or events may occur as was 'planned' in the soul vision, but we are not helpless to either make or prevent it from being so. It is my belief that when we do find ourselves, consciously or not, at a point that mirrors a segment of our soul vision, we experience that sense of dejavu, or improbable coincidence and such experiences probably become more frequent when we begin following closely to the journey set out for ourselves in our soul visions. To be clear, by 'experience' here I do not mean that we see miraculous things occur, though perhaps that may happen for some. But for me, one such coincidence may be the simple appearance of an improbable person, animal, plant, or object at an improbable time which happens to beneficial; a profound and enlightening comment someone makes in passing; the divulgence of necessary wisdom or information at just the right time; or just a feeling that makes you smile and think: 'huh, neat'.

This is what I believe to be true. This is what I would describe to be my full set of beliefs, more or less. This is how I would feel confident defining myself, religiously or spiritually. It is an elaborate system, one which I do not expect anyone to share in its entirety. It has many links to other religions, spiritual philosophies, and peoples' ideas, and at the same time it is completely my own. Who I am is in part innate, but much of me has been sculpted by my experiences and interactions with other people, animals, plants, places, and events. No one else has lived my life or shared step for step my experiences, so no one's values or beliefs *should* be exactly like mine. My perception of the world and my location in the universe is unique to me, and was formed by my relation to the universal 'string' of energy and the many 'layers' of that which I believe to be a single whole. How could I possibly sum everything I believe as I have just described, into one word? How can any of the terms Christian, Muslim, Taoist, Buddhist or Hindu be represen-tative of what those billions of people believe? This is what I see as problematic with categorizing and titling religious beliefs. I would argue there are billions of variations from 'general' belief sets to be expected, equal or greater than the num-ber of people alive today. Our beliefs are significantly more complex than any sin-gle term can explain, and so they require equally intricate descriptions instead of broad or simple titles.

A Connection? Animal Cruelty & Human Slavery.

I believe that the mustang is a highly trainable animal that can serve many purposes within today's horse industry. There is no question that they can be trained to become trustworthy partners for horse people, providing years of service, entertainment and companionship. However, I am just as strong in my belief that, if poorly treated, they can become dangerous and destructive. Wild mustangs should never be taken for granted by ill-prepared people who do not understand the level of competence necessary for dealing with a wild animal. I believe that equus in general is an often-misunderstood species and is, sadly, treated by many human beings in an unfair manner. When you add the aspects of non-domestic and wild to this scenario, the level of mis-understanding seems to increase significantly.

—Monty Roberts[1]

In this section I will start by focusing on Aristotle's thoughts, published in Tom Regan and Peter Singer's anthology, "Animals in the History of Western Thought: Part One" from *Animal Rights and Human Obligations*. I intend to articulate the connection between attitudes and behaviors involved in animal cruelty and slavery, and point out specific connection with the relationship humans have with horses. Western culture does not tolerate slavery and racism today, but speciesism is perfectly acceptable. I want to point out that the state of mind, attitudes and behaviors which justify slavery are very much the same as those that justify animal cruelty. Aristotle makes what some call the "dreaded comparison" but what I feel to be quite accurate in fact, connecting the treatment of animals with the treatment of slaves.

---

1. Monty Roberts, *Monty Roberts.com* "News & Information—Monty Talks About Mustangs," http://www.montyroberts.com/news/stories/news_stry_mustangs.html

First, I think it necessary to explain the perspective from which I approach the issue. "No one has the right to say 'you do what I tell you, or I'll hurt you.'"[2] (Monty Roberts). This quote coupled with the eco-feminist belief in a non-hierarchical society, which presupposes oppression, define what I believe: that no amount of human supremacy should be tolerable. I value animal life just as much as I value human life, and do not agree that forcing any living being into submission is right or justifiable. Whether you agree or disagree with this perspective, I ask that you adopt it for the duration of this section of my book in order to be able to fully understand the comparisons and connections between human slavery and animal cruelty that are so obvious to me, in my own Western culture.

Aristotle said, "It is clear that the rule of the soul over the body, and of the mind the rational element over the passionate, is natural and expedient; whereas the equality of the two or the rule of the inferior is always hurtful."[3] He goes on to explain his belief that it is only natural for some humans to be superior to others, and the consequential development of master and slave relationship is entirely justified. He proposes that people are better off this way, and explains that the same is true for animals in relation to people. He says, ".... tame animals have a better nature than wild, and all tame animals are better off when they are ruled by man; for then they are preserved."[4]

While it may be difficult for us to comprehend that it was actually believed (or at least believed for the purpose of justification by those in the position of power) that those held as slaves were actually better off in a constant state of submission, we need to consider our opinions regarding these same justifications surrounding how we feel about the animals we call our pets. In all honesty, many people do believe that their pets should be grateful to be supplied with food, water and shelter, because they do not believe their animals could survive on their own. In most cases this is far from true, but we choose to believe it anyway because it is a convenient justification for us to "own" our pets and be able to discipline them as we see fit—when they have an "accident" in the house, for example.

Aristotle states, "again, the male is by nature superior, and the female inferior; and the one rules, and the other is ruled; this principle, of necessity, extends to all mankind."[5] This was the mindset of the time, again probably difficult for most of

---

2. Monty Roberts, *Monty Roberts.com* "Join-Up international", http://www.montyroberts.com/jui_about.html

3. *Animals in the History of Western Thought: Part One*, 2nd Ed. From "Animal Rights and Human Obligations", edited by Tom Regan and Peter Singer, 1989, 4.

4. Ibid., 4.

5. Ibid., 4

us who were raised in a modern household to comprehend, but when applied to the way we regard animals, it isn't quite as foreign. A direct connection to slavery comes when Aristotle said:

> Where then there is such a difference as that between soul and body, or between men and animals, (as in the case of those whose business is to use their body, and who can do nothing better), the lower sort are by nature slaves, and it is better for them as for all inferiors that they should be under rule of a master. For he who can be, and therefore is, another's and he who participates in rational principle enough to apprehend, but not to have, such a principle, is a slave by nature. Whereas the lower animals cannot even apprehend a principle; they obey their instincts. ***And indeed the use made of slaves and of tame animals is not very different; for both their bodies minister to the needs of life*** ... [6]

The above quote is quite powerful because it is incredibly difficult for us to accept as truth, and yet it was strange for someone to think any different in the time this was written. Again, in comparison to the matter of how we treat animals even in our "modern" culture today, we hold very much the same belief that it is "only natural" for animals to be considered inferior to humans, and that they must, in most circumstances, "earn their keep" by contributing to the production of the "necessities of life". Be this the milk produced by a cow, the eggs produced a chicken, or the safety ensured by the guard of a dog, it is common perspective in our culture that animals were put on the earth to serve humans as we see fit. How then can we truly say that we cannot comprehend even some of the mindset of human slavery? Is it not the very same thing to flaunt superiority over one living being as it is to do the same to another? Is it not just as cruel and unnecessary to abuse an innocent animal as it is to do the same to a human being? Is it not the same wrong to force an animal into submission and work as it is to do the same to a human? Is it not the same evil to inflict unnecessary and undeserved pain and suffering on one living being as it is another? Where then, is the difference between human slavery and animal slavery?

Certainly not everyone who owns an animal abuses that position, but it does happen quite often, and our culture thinks almost nothing of it. Is that not a bit hypocritical of us? Similarly, not every slave was treated with constant cruelty, but the fact that they were considered slaves, and inferior to another is an example of evil, by the definition as follows:

---

6.   Ibid., 4-5. Emphasis added.

Evil: intentional cause or infliction of any unnecessary pain and/or suffering to any living being, human or non-human.

One could easily compare the common modern attitudes toward, and treatment of just about any animal to the human slavery that took place in Western history, but for the purpose of this written contemplation, I believe the most vivid comparison is with the horse in particular. Just as many families from the "old South" established their success and fortunes on the backs of slaves, our ancestors established "western civilization" on the backs of horses. They were first shipped here from Europe with explorers, and those who survived shipwrecks or escaped soon banded together to form the herds of wild mustangs whose descendents continue to roam what is left of unsettled North America. The first settlers also brought domestic horses from Europe, and soon those from the wild North American herds were being captured and used as well. (The image of horse-drawn covered wagon trains is easily accessible to just about every imagination.) Not only did the horses provide transportation for the humans themselves, but also their belongings and their efforts were required to carve out those first roads as well. It is common knowledge that once on a plot of land a settler chose to call his own, the horses were put to work clearing the land, hauling trees to build the homes, and tilling the fields for crops. Their partnership with man was absolutely necessary for Western development to occur as quickly as it did, but can it really be called a partnership horses had with humans?

Let's consider first, the training methods humans used to acquire this partnership with the powerful animal their survival, or at the very least their quality of life, depended upon. The traditional "cowboy" method of training a horse in the "old West" is called "breaking." The term refers to the intentional breaking of the horse's spirit, as well as the common consequence of broken bones, both the horses' and sometimes the trainers'. These were the results of pounds of rope and equipment tied to the terrified horses without any attempt to desensitize the instinctive flight animals to these foreign materials first. Brute force and fear are the main tools in training horses and compelling them to work for us—exactly what was used against slaves.

As a flight animal it is the horses' natural instinct to first run away from anything that poses a potential threat to them and *then*, from a safe distance, check out whatever it was that appeared threatening. This is how their species learned to survive in the wild. But our Western ancestors, exactly like many cowboys or trainers of today, used fences and corrals to prevent horses from doing what allows them to calm down naturally in a frightful situation, and investigate a situation on their own terms. Instead, horses are forced to run frantically in enclosed areas, often in a terrified attempt to get away from the trainer/owner.

The "breaking" process generally includes a period of "sacking out" the horse. This is accomplished a number of ways and the particulars are only specific to the trainer and materials available. The idea is to first tie up the horse so that he/she can hardly move. Their heads will often be tied in place so they cannon rear or back up, and are only able to try to move from side to side to get away. Their hind legs are tied up as well, to prevent them from kicking with full force, and it is not uncommon for one hind leg to be tied up, off the ground so the horse is forced to balance on three legs, and essentially hop away from whatever objects the trainer approaches him/her with. Once the horse has been tied to the trainer's standards he/she is approached with any number of objects the trainer chooses. The intent of this process is to desensitize the horse to new objects; the common outcome of the process is an exhausted, and terrified animal who has been severely traumatized and more often than not, injured in one way or another, from a rope burn on their skin, to a muscle, joint or bone injury from constant falls in their struggle with the ropes to get away. The process is supposed to continue until the horse stops trying to kick at and move away from the object–this is achieved not because the horse has become used to the object or been made to understand that it isn't going to hurt him/her, but because the horse has no more strength or energy left to try and flee the situation that it gives up. This is just one step in the process of "training" a horse's spirit out of him/her.

As this method of "training" progresses a horse must learn to stop when the human says "Whoa". What many trainers use for this section of training is another system of ropes tied to the horse. This is called a "running W." It consists of ropes tied to the horses' legs, just above their hooves, not always all four legs, but always at least the front two. These ropes are long and the ends not tied to the horse are held by the trainer. As the horse moves around the training area the trainer will say "whoa" at random, and simultaneously stop moving himself, fixing the ropes in place, pulling the horse's feet out from under him/her causing him/her to fall on his chest and head. Not only is this a psychologically shocking, frustrating and traumatizing experience, but considering the average horse weighs at least 700 pounds, this is a very physically dangerous training technique for the horse, and in the end, is not very effective.

Riding techniques derived from training techniques such as these also use aggressive equipment and employ tools of force, fear and pain to achieve the desired goal of the rider. Spurs, crops, whips and harsh bits are all commonly used to "manage" a "difficult" horse in order to make him/her eventually become submissive–the ultimate goal of most riders/trainers who use such techniques. Sadly, this mindset is not even a relatively new one, nor is it as harsh or cruel as some techniques that were developed earlier.

> ... The trainer [should] calmly inspire confidence in the horse and that each horse be treated as an individual.
>
> Contemporary Englishmen thought otherwise. Thomas Blundeville recommended that riders be equipped to deal with recalcitrant horses: as iron bar set with prickles would be suspended from the horse's tail and passed between the horse's legs by a cord. The rider could thus draw the cord up and mete out punishment whenever he saw fit. If this failed, Blundeville advised, "let a footman stand behind you with a shrewd cat tied at one end of a long pole with her belly upwards, so as she may have mouth and claws at liberty. And when your horse may stay or go backwards, let him thrust the cat between his legs so as she may scratch and bite him, sometimes by the thighs, sometimes by the rump and often times by the stones.[7]

It surprises me to consider that most of the successful and well known trainers through history believed that "fear and anger had no place in the training of horses" and yet so few "common" trainers follow suit. The best trainers use patience and listen to what the horse they work with says to them–they take the time to get the training done that each individual horse requires to feel safe and comfortable and learn to trust. Yet much more often, at least in western cultures, horses are subjected to trainers who hurriedly attempt to "break" a number of horses simultaneously. I can't help but agree wholeheartedly with the eighteenth century, Duke of Newcastle who wrote:

> A boy is a long time before he knows his alphabet, and longer before he has learned to spell, and perhaps several years before he can read distinctly; and yet there are some people who, as soon as they get on a young horse, entirely undressed and untaught, fancy that by beating and spurring they will make him a dressed horse in one morning. I would fain ask such stupid people whether by beating a boy they would teach him to read without first showing him the alphabet? Sure, they would beat him to death, before they would make him read.[8]

---

7. Lawrence Scanlan, *Wild About Horses: Our Timeless Passion for the Horse*, Random House of Canada Ltd., 1998, 92.
8. Ibid., 92.

This is much closer to the line of thinking more humane and gentle trainers hold. Now let's consider a method of training horses that has proven to be exponentially more successful on a number of levels for both the horse and trainer that was actually developed by horses themselves–sort of. An American man named Monty Roberts was born and raised on a horse ranch, where he not only witnessed his father "break" dozens of horses every year through the methods described above, but he was also forced to use the same techniques as a boy. He couldn't help but think that there had to be a better, more kind and gentle way to achieve the same goal with horses and has devoted his life to sharing and teaching the method that he found as a boy. Monty spent many of his summers in the Nevada high dessert just observing herds of wild mustangs, their interaction with each other and predators. He witnessed the culture of horses and was able to learn their silent language which he calls "equus." This is a language composed entirely of body positioning and eye contact and Monty taught himself to communicate with horses using this, their own language. He uses the same simple "dialogue" to "start" every horse and more often than not accomplishes within one hour (and without any aspect of violence or aggression) that which would take most trainers days or even weeks to accomplish.

His tried and true method is called "join-up" and the only equipment used for the entire process include: two cotton long lines, thirty feet long, a snaffle bit (one of the most gentle bits available), a saddle pad and saddle, yourself and a haltered horse. (A round pen makes the job easier but is not necessary; preferable dimensions are fifty feet or sixteen meters in diameter with eight foot high walls.) The step-by-step instructions to achieving join-up with a horse are described by Monty Roberts as follows:

> Bring the horse, with his halter on, into the pen and have with you one long-line. Stand near the center of the pen and introduce yourself by rubbing with the flat of your hand (no patting) the horse's forehead, even if you are already acquainted. Now move away toward the rear of the horse, staying out of the kick zone.

> When you are behind the animal or when he flees–whichever comes first– pitch the line toward his rear quarters. This light sash (long-line) cannot hurt him in any way. At this point, almost all young horses will take flight and proceed around the pen. The horse is retreating so you must advance. Keep the pressure on. Pitch the line about two times per revolution or whatever it takes to keep your subject retreating.

Maintain an aggressive mode: Your eyes drilled on his eyes, your shoulder axis square with his head. Maintain forward movement as much as possible, but do not enter his kick zone. Try to get the horse to canter five or six revolutions one way; then reverse and repeat, except that this time you are readying the horse for a message: Would he like to stop all this work?

Particularly watch the inside ear (the ear, that is, closest to you in the center of the pen). That ear will slow up its movement or stop moving altogether, while the outside ear will continue to monitor his surroundings. The head will begin to tip, ears to inside, and the neck will bend slightly to bring his head closer to the center of the circle. He will probably lick and chew, running his tongue outside the mouth.

Finally, he should crane his head down near the ground. The ear gives you respect. Coming closer means just that. Licking and chewing says, "I am a flight animal, and I'm eating so I can't fear you." Craning the head down means, "If we could have a meeting to renegotiate, I would let you be chairman." Experience will sharpen your senses to this communication, but essentially when you observe the horse in this mode, he is asking you to take the pressure off. He wants to stop.

Now coil the line and assume a submissive mode, with your eyes down. Do not look at his eyes. Bring your shoulder axis to a forty-five degree position. This is an invitation for him to come to you, or at least look your way and stop retreating. If he will come to you this is good! If he stands and faces you but does not move forward, then start to move closer to him, but do it in arcs or semicircles, not straight at him.

If he leaves you, put him back to work for a few more laps. Then repeat the process. As you move closer, do it with your shoulder axis at forty-five degree angles to his body axis. For the most part, show your back to him. He should voluntarily move toward you and reach out with his nose to your shoulders. This is *join-up*.[9]

Following these steps, a saddle and bridle are secured on the horse and the same process is repeated until the horse is comfortable with the new appendages. The last step is for a rider to lay his weight on the back of the horse, and then sit in the saddle for the very first ride, again following the same join-up process in the round-pen. That is the entire process of Monty Robert's *Joint-Up* as explained in his book "The Man Who Listens to Horses." He developed this technique as a

---

9.   Monty Roberts, *The Man Who Listens to Horses*, Vintage Canada, of Random House of Canada Ltd., 1998, Appendix, 233-234.

boy watching mustangs roam the desert in Nevada and has refined it over the years, but he first recognized this particular dialogue while observing a dominant mare discipline a young colt within one of these wild herds. The mare was reprimanding the colt for his aggressive behavior toward other horses in the herd that was obviously frustrating them. She had literally run at the colt, forcing him out of and away from the protection of the herd and maintained the aggressive body position Monty assumes in Join Up, with her chest square to the colt, her eyes focused on his. The colt raced around the outside of the herd, searching for a way back into it, but the mare refused to let him re-enter the herd until he had communicated with her in exactly the same way Monty looks for the horse to communicate with him in the round pen. Once the colt was allowed back into his herd the mare groomed him and showed him a great deal of affection, praising him for his change of attitude and welcoming him back to the group.

This is essentially what Monty's intent is. He understands that horses are herd animals, and feel uncomfortable and vulnerable when they are isolated from their herd. This is why he uses a round pen, and the same body language as a dominant mare in a herd–he sends the horse away from him and then offers (in the language natural to the horse) to let the horse enter into his herd on the condition that he is given respect. When Join Up takes place successfully the horse is more than willing to follow you and trusts you to place equipment like tack and rider on his back because you have become his herd and safe place. This is an incredibly beautiful and perhaps one of the most moving and inspirational forms of interaction to witness or experience between a human and horse. It is absolute communication that requires unlimited patience and complete trust and honesty–what could be more beautiful than such a perfect partnership?

It is important to note Monty's thoughts about this process in terms of respecting and understanding the horse as well:

> It should be plain that starting horses gently is easy, efficient, and systematic: it is freely available to anyone with a positive attitude who is not frightened of horses. The first requirement is that you discard any preconceived notions about starting your horse. Do retain, however, all your experiences with the horse that have taught you not to fear him and that enable you to move around him safely and effectively.
>
> Hold in your mind the idea that the horse can do no wrong; that any action taken by the horse–especially the young unstarted horse–was most likely influenced by you. We can do little to teach the horse; we can only create an environment in which he can learn. Likewise with people: the student who has knowledge pushed into his brain learns little, but he can absorb a great deal

when he chooses to learn.... If we refuse to believe that the horse can communicate, pain can be used to train him somewhat effectively. But pain is needless and terribly limiting.[10]

To compare even this process with our culture's history of human slavery, Monty's ideas are relatively new to the horse world and still widely rejected by even some of the biggest people in the horse industry. They refuse to acknowledge the alternative, or bother to take the time to teach themselves something new, and instead remain ignorant to a way of doing things that would be much less demanding or stressful for both themselves and their horses. Change in the attitude of the general "horse public" is beginning to come to acknowledge and respect Monty's techniques as reliable, but it is slow to catch on everywhere; just as a change in the attitude of the plantation owners from the "old South" did not come quickly or easily. (Nor has such a change in Southern attitudes come entirely, even to this day.) Monty faced rejection and even personal emotional and physical abuse from his own father for suggesting his new way of doing things. He has a number of dedicated and serious apprentices, but there are a lot more people who refuse to give up the "traditional" way of working with horses that are inevitably working against him in his goal to leave the world a better place for horses.

Now, let's look at the methods used to capture wild horses in the West. As our technology has advanced, so have our "herding" methods. Helicopters have been used to scare wild horses into the open and across the land where trucks would join in this incredibly unfair chase, sometimes adding to the horses' terror with the use of guns:

> The mustangs are driven at breakneck speed by planes from their meager refuge in the rough and barren rimrock onto flatlands or dry lake beds. There the chase is taken up by hunters standing on the fast-moving pickup trucks ... after a run of fifteen to twenty miles, the horses, many of them carrying bullet wounds inflicted to make them run faster, are easy victims for ropers.[11]

After this, the horses are lassoed. Bleeding from their noses because they have been breathing so hard from running, their feet are tied together and they are dragged up ramps, (often stripping the hide from their flanks) onto stock trailers where are untied and prodded to their feet. The ones too young, or too badly injured to load are left behind to die.

---

10.   Roberts, *The Man Who Listens to Horses*: Appendix, 231.
11.   Scanlan, *Wild About Horses*, 48.

Sadly this is one of the least malicious and selfish methods that are regularly employed by humans to round up herds of wild horses to "control" their populations:

> The cruelty was methodical, even ingenious. In *America's Last Wild Horses*, Hope Ryden describes how mustangers in Wyoming's Red Desert would capture and gentle a mare, then sew her nostrils almost completely shut with rawhide or barbed wire. Unable to take in a full breath of air, her speed was reduced and she would act as a brake on the herd in the spring when another roundup occurred. Another braking tactic was to bend a horseshoe around the ankle of a mare which bruised her when she ran. Only a quality mare was selected, wrote Ryden–"so she could perform double duty by bearing a good colt for the mustangers during the year she was free on the desert.[12]

The brutality of these actions, and the often horrific results are absolutely appalling, completely unnecessary and entirely avoidable: Many mustangs, especially foals, forced to run over such hard ground for such extended distances have virtually nothing left of their feet by the time they are allowed to stop, despite the high quality of their hoof structure and strength. Or their feet are so badly injured that some of these magnificent creatures must be destroyed.

These animals who are often regarded as a symbol of freedom and Western heritage are considered no more than pests who compete with livestock herds for water, grasslands, and hay by cattle ranchers and sheep farmers. Today the wild horse herds in North America consist of less than 40,000 individuals when less than 200 years ago anywhere from two to five million horses roamed free on the plains of our continent–this dramatic decrease in population can only be attributed to human interference–and yet farmers are still complaining that there are too many! Perhaps populations need management to ensure the health of the horses when considering the serious lack of resources humans allow them access to, but there are obviously much more humane methods of accomplishing such tasks. Consider this story:

> One morning in 1950, Velma Bronn Johnston was driving along Highway 359 to work in Reno when a truck hauling horses cut in front of her car. Shocked by a stream of blood dripping from the truck, she followed the van to a slaughterhouse and watched from behind bushes as a yearling was trampled to a pulp between terrified stallions. The horses had buckshot wounds; some stood on bloody stumps after their hooves had worn off from running over

---

12.   Ibid., 49-50.

rocks; one stallion had his eyes shot out. What Johnston saw and heard that day would change her life. She would take on the U.S. federal government, specifically the Bureau of Land Management (BLM), which was encharged with managing wild-horse populations.[13]

This woman played a big part in saving wild North American horses from extinction. Her self, and a number of other individuals working together would eventually have the slaughter of wild horses outlawed in the United States of America. To the horror of true horse lovers, this law was recently lifted as the BLM proposed a plan to further reduce wild horse populations from the existing 37,000 to 28,000 before the end of the year 2005. There is talk of wild horse adoption programs being established to locate homes for all of these animals, but with the current over abundance of already domesticated horses for the "consumer demand" in North America, finding homes for another 9,000 untrained and very much independent horses is a ridiculous proposition, far from realistic!

So, (not all, but the majority of) wild horses are captured, abused or terrified in "training" sessions that force them into submission, and then sold for profit at auctions. After they are purchased the horses are sentenced to an uncertain fate; they could have relatively kind owners, or ones who think of them and treat them like machines, designed and born to do whatever work their human owner tells them to do, few will be lucky enough to go to homes where they will be appreciated for what they were, and respected for their own intelligence and individuality. Any that are lucky enough to be returned to the wild, unwanted at auction, are only be sentenced to the possibility of a repeat experience of the trauma and torture they had just suffered. Does this not resemble much of what happened with the slaves purchased in our Western culture after they had been taken captive as a result of a difference in the availability and level of technology between Black Africans and their White suppressors? How can we say with such confidence then, that what we did to slaves then was wrong but what we do to animals today is acceptable?

Intentionally inflicting unnecessary pain and suffering on another living being, be they human or non-human animal is the definition of what I believe to be evil. The relevance of this comparison is to point out that the same evil behavior our culture deemed unacceptable toward humans is often overlooked when it is done to animals. Studies have proven that this is a dangerous situation, because violence towards animals often increases the likelihood of developing violence toward humans. We need to consider the issue of speciesism as well. This is what Peter Singer explains to be the belief that only beings of the same species, or at

---

13. Ibid., 46-47.

the very least with a number of specific characteristics of one species—human, have a moral worth. Arguments that prove racism to be wrong should prove speciesism to be equally wrong, but for those who do not believe humans and animals to have the same moral worth are, by definition, speciesists. Again I ask, is that not rather hypocritical?

So, with that in mind we need to think seriously about what beliefs and behaviors should be acceptable in our society. We need to consider the hypocrisy of a society that ignores arguments against speciesism and justifies cruelty to non-human animals but claims to believe racism is wrong and cruelty to humans is unjust; after all, humans are animals too. What then, is the potential of this hypocritical society to begin to ignore their beliefs about human moral worth and begin to treat each other with cruelty in order to improve the quality of individual human lives … again? If we can justify cruelty to animals and speciesism now, what is the potential for our society to begin to accept racism and human slavery … again?

Before we act let's first consider the consequences that will inevitably be endured if we fulfill those actions. Let's consider first the waste of beautiful and invaluable life of these incredible creatures if we sentence them to death simply because we decide that now we want the land they have called their home for hundreds of years for our own use. Let's consider first the incredible loss of intelligence we must face by destroying these innocent, honest, genuine and truly complex animals. Let's first consider the loss of a truly unique and incomparable therapy that horses willingly provide to children and adults alike with all sorts of mental, intellectual and physical challenges, with only patience, understanding and compassion, and never judgment. Let's first consider exactly what it is we are regarding as simple pests, and acknowledge the truly beautiful gift of love, companionship and wisdom we seem so eager to overlook and destroy. Once we have considered all of these things and only then, should we make a decision about the horses whose fate ultimately lies in our hands.

> To see a stallion and mare affectionately groom each other, amid the man-height sagebrush of Wyoming's silent Red Desert, fills me with awe. And, if there is anything more beautiful on this earth than standing alone in an Assateague marsh in a cold March sunset, watching a band of brown and white pintos graze peacefully while snow geese glide overhead and sika deer gracefully prance through on their way to some favorite feeding place, I want to discover it before my own journey is finished. I am riches, beyond description, because of these events.

And *that* is the value of a wild horse.

—*Into the Wind* by Jay F. Kirkpatrick (emphasis in original)

Vibrational Medicine & Animal Consciousness

The Bible does not say a lot about our treatment of animals, and what it does say is both contradictory and can be interpreted in several different ways. In the book of Genesis it says that people have dominion over everything living on the earth, but the definition of the word 'dominion' is controversial. It could be taken to mean that people have dominance and superiority over all living things, or it could mean that people have a responsibility to care for and tend to all of these things. There are a number of other passages that suggest God gave humans animals for food, and then others that say to treat animals as we would treat other humans, and that to kill another human is wrong. So it is obvious there is no distinct explanation provided by the Bible that tells us how to treat animals properly.

Aristotle proposed a justification for the ill treatment, or human use and consumption of animals' flesh, byproducts and labour by comparing animals to slaves, which was "only natural" in his time. Aristotle believed that slavery was right and justified because some people were "naturally superior to others" and connected this belief to the way humans use animals with much the same attitude, that humans are "naturally superior to animals, and therefore have the right to use them as we please."[1] Obviously Western culture has come to realize that slavery is not natural, nor should it be justified in any way, and was outlawed. Perhaps the same perspective will be adopted with regard to the use of animals in the future.

Saint Thomas Aquinas believed in different kinds of souls, the Vegetative Soul and the Rational Soul. The former he believed every living thing to possess, because it was simply the state of a living existence. The Rational Soul on the other hand, Aquinas only believed humans to have because we know that we are capable of thought. Aquinas did not believe that animals could think. He formed his justification for what we do to them around this belief and he explained that

---

1.   *Animals in the History of Western Thought*, 4-5.

wherever the Bible seems to tell us not to be cruel to animals, it is only there to make people kinder to each other, because violence toward animals tends to spread to violence toward people.[2] If with nothing else, Aquinas was right in this as a number of studies have proved; learning to treat animals kindly tends to result in making people kinder to one another, as seen in programs between imprisoned criminals and SPCA's. The same is true for the opposite, where abusive spouses and/or parents also tend to be abusive toward animals.

Renee Descartes was perhaps the biggest opponent of animal rights activists. He believed animals to be merely automata; that they looked and acted as if they feel pain, but they do not really because there are just like nature's machinery, their biological systems no different from the dials and systems of a clock. He rationalized this by explaining that non-human animals are capable of human speech, parrots for example, however they do not tell us their thoughts. This he held to determine that they have no thoughts, and then, if they have no thoughts he concluded they must be unable to feel pain. He and his set of beliefs lead to a number of animal experimentations, and the development of vivisection. This is the practice of immobilizing an animal and cutting it open while it is still alive and without any form of sedation or pain relief. He justified these horribly cruel actions toward animals by denying the fact that they have thoughts, consciousness and awareness or ability of feeling pain.[3]

Bentham is known for utilitarianism, a model of morality that defines good from bad by assigning every effect/outcome of an action with a number to calculate in the end and determine whether the good outweigh the bad. He suggests that it is not a question of whether animals can reason or talk, but whether they can suffer that should determine how we should treat them.[4] And animals can indeed suffer.

The overall theme of attitudes towards animals in the Western tradition has been a constant effort to justify why we continue to do the things we do to animals that obviously causes pain and suffering, by denying the fact that they are able to feel these things. The theme has been in Western thinking that humans are superior to animals, and therefore have the right to use them however we please, and rationalize or justify this by looking for ways that non-human animals are different from humans, refusing to believe or acknowledge many obvious flaws with these proposals.

---

2.   *Animals in the History of Western Thought*, 6-12.
3.   *Animals in the History of Western Thought*, 13-19.
4.   *Animals in the History of Western Thought*, 25-26.

So the Animal Rights debate has roots as far back as with philosophers of the centuries B.C.E. and intensified in the 1700s when Europeans, British in particular, began questioning and opposing vivisection and has continued with the development of organizations like the Society for the Prevention of Cruelty to Animals. It has become more of a popular movement in recent years, and there are several different levels of support. There are Animal Welfare Supporters, different degrees of Animal Rights supporters, and then Animal Liberationists who are at the most extreme end of the continuum.

The position of the animal welfare group is that animals do have some moral standing but that they have no rights. This determines that animal experimentation is okay, but abusing or mistreating them unnecessarily is wrong. The welfare of the animal is the primary consideration of this group, and they believe there are some restrictions on what we can do to/with animals. Michael Fox is a representative of this group, and wrote a book about his beliefs. He says that animals are not in our moral sphere because they are not like us. Because they cannot include us in their moral sphere, we don't have to include them in ours. He believes that animals have no inner consciousness, and that they are like unconscious humans.

Peter Singer is perhaps the most famous animal liberationist as he has some rather controversial ideas regarding experiment patients. This group believes in the principle of equality, and the fact that animals do suffer and should have a moral value. Singer often references "speciesism" which as we have seen before, is the discrimination against different species than your own. There are two kinds of speciesism according to Singer; Bare and Indirect. Bare speciesism is defined by the belief that anything not of the human species has no moral worth, while Indirect speciesism defines the moral state of a member of any species by its possession of certain human-like characteristics. Singer suggests that some animals may indeed have more moral worth than a handicapped or senile human, because they are more able to have meaningful relationships. This is the group of people who often free or 'liberate' animals from experimentation or factory farming, etc. Singer admits that he, as a liberationist, is not the same as an animal rights activist because he does not believe in the idea of rights, for animals or for humans.

The Animal Rights group believes animals to have the right not to experience unnecessary pain and suffering inflicted on them. They believe that these rights should not be taken away, even if it is to help humans. This does not mean that animals should have full humans rights, these people do not believe animals should be given the vote, for example, but it means that animals have a worth simply because they are subjects of life, and they have emotions and feelings, etc.

This group believes that animals' worth is inherent just as is humans'. The very same argument against racism are therefore applicable to speciesism, and should convince people that this is just as wrong. Tom Regan is an Animal Rights activist, and argued that a vegetarian lifestyle is the only justifiable one in certain situations, because it provides a healthy existence for the human participant, and does not unnecessarily take the life of an animal.

A less radical sect of the animal rights group could be dubbed Animal RightsLITE[5] which agrees that speciesism is a bad thing and that Animals have rights. However, this group does not believe that animals have the same rights as humans. R.G. Frey is a representative of this group, and he explains that from this perspective, animal experimentation is alright, as long as we can justify it. He believes that the value of human quality of life is higher than that of an animal. In order to value animal and human life equally, there would have to be experimentation of humans. To this, Peter Singer agreed whole heartedly, and proposed experimenting on the "marginal cases" of human life—the ones that resemble the description Descartes would have proposed of animals. Those humans who cannot communicate through speech and are unconscious, are therefore by Descartes' definition, not be able to feel pain. At least in these experiments there would have to be no animal to human estimated extrapolation of results, as there is with animal experimentation which is the point Singer's proposal sought to make—if we can justify some treatment for non-human animals then we should be able to justify the same treatment for humans as well to keep with the speciesism ideology.

Clearly, the debate over non-human animal consciousness, rights, and experimentation is, by nature, multidimensional. Science, religion, philosophy, culture, rights, values, and ethics are all important contributors. Fundamental questions involved seek to determine whether or not 'they' are similar or different from 'us' biologically, and mentally. Can they feel pain and suffer like us? And is it still ethical, either way, for us to use and subject them to experimental cruelties for a *chance* at medical or commercial gains/advances for ourselves?

Before anything else we often look to the evidence of science, biology and/or medicine in particular to determine whether or not there exists the anatomical congruence between 'them' and 'us' to make any experimental research viable and/or relevant for us in the end. Only after investigating that sub-debate do most people begin to explore the idea of non-human animal consciousness and the 'mental stuff' that allows us to think. This comes from a different plain of

---

5.   I must credit my professor Dr. Robinson for the creation of this term.

existence, and is a complex area of thought and debate in and of itself. It represents and encompasses the 'mind-body problem'.

So, after the first two sub-debates are investigated one moves on to the subject of rights–human and non. For some, like Peter Singer rights shouldn't exist at all, for anyone. But for everyone who accepts the concept of 'rights' for the matters of animal experimentation and consciousness they must necessarily reflect on the value and measure of individual 'rights' in a scaled sense. By this I mean that in order to engage completely in the animal experimentation debate one must contemplate what the value of different rights are in comparison to others. But how do you measure something that is considered an inherent or fundamental 'right'? How is any one 'right' more important than another if they are both 'rights'? That said, how do you equate anything to the 'right' to life? As all of this illustrates, the animal experimentation and consciousness debate is an incredibly complex and multifaceted one. The purpose of this section will be to explore each of these core questions briefly, then investigate two holistic healing practices/ approaches–Bach Flower Essences and Reiki–and what they contribute to this debate.

So, let's start at the beginning. But what is that? When thinking about anatomy and the mind it is a bit of a chicken and egg conundrum–which came first? No one is sure of the answer to this, but we 'know' more about the physical body than the mental 'stuff' scientifically, so let's begin there. The whole field of biology within science contributes to our understanding of our physical selves and we have collected a significant amount of knowledge over the generations on how our bodies 'work'. The medicine and medical practices we have are quite advanced to date, but that is not to say what existed in the past was irrelevant or insignificant.

Consider that Plato wrote in *The Republic*:

> The cure of the part should not be attempted without treatment of the whole. No attempt should be made to cure the body without the soul, and, if the head and body are to be healthy, you must begin by curing the mind ... For this is the great error of our day in the treatment of the human body, that physicians first separate the soul from the body.

It seems the ancients were aware of the important balance between mind, body, and soul which 'New Age' medicines are promoting today. While scientists and philosophers debate over what the mind, body and soul *are*, healers through the ages have recognized the three as a necessary triad for life, all of which need to be addressed and incorporated in true healing, where health is established when these three are balanced. The type of holistic medicine or therapy that specifically works with intentions to balance and heal each of the mind, body and soul together is called Vibrational Medicine.

> Wholism must be recognized and implemented in our lives on many levels. We have been fragmented for too long in our materialistic, mechanistic, scientific worldview that has been the determining factor in our reality … It is now time to put the pieces back together and acknowledge that we are multidimensional beings, a complex of body, mind, and spirit intertwined.[6]

Vibrational Medicine is based on the concept that "we are much more than physical beings, that in fact at our inner most core we are energetic beings … healing practices [are] directed towards this subtle energy field where mind, body, and spirit merged."[7] The idea with this type of medicine is that we are physical beings last, and we exist primarily in the mind and soul such that when there is dis-ease in either of these two elements of our life that is not rebalanced quickly, our physical body is last in responding with the manifestation of what we know as 'disease'. Essentially, the body is viewed as an earthly vessel, which comes alive when inhabited by a soul which moves through the mind. According to the theories of vibrational medicine our mind, body and soul are simply energies that are resonating together in our physical life experience. When the three are balanced and in harmony with each other we are healthy. When any of the energies is out of alignment with the others, it is the cause of dis-ease in the energy harmony and the individual's highest good; this is the root of disease and sickness or ill health according to vibrational medicine theory. Subsequently, it is the focus of what and where healing needs to take place in order to achieve true or optimal health. If we stop after only treating the physical symptoms, or mask them with a drug of some kind, the root of the problem will persist and continue to negatively effect the whole being and result in recurring physical health problems.

The basic premise is that there is a higher purpose to life than merely existing. So, when we are off-track from that higher goal, purpose, or good in our life there is an imbalance in our energy resonances. There is value in emotions in correlation to health here. The more negative emotional states/moods we experience, the more negative energy flows with/to our body, mind, and soul energies which subsequently carries negative affects. The same, but opposite is true of positive

---

6.   Rachel Hasnas, *The Essence of Bach Flowers*, (California: The Crossing Press, 1999), 11.
7.   Ibid., 16.

moods. This suggests our moods can directly influence our emotional, mental and physical health, and it is what vibrational medicine seeks to treat.

> Humanity has lost touch with this ancient wisdom. For centuries we have been indoctrinated with a medical model that sees the body as a machine. In the last few decades the old paradigm has begun to be seriously challenged with the advent of mind-body medicine. That our thoughts and feelings play a significant part in determining our state of health is once again acknowledged.
>
> Traditional Western medicine is beginning to recognize that when we are emotionally upset or mentally distressed, our health suffers. The old model can't explain this. Medical scientists are now discovering that there are other factors beyond the physical that must also be addressed.
>
> To this end, a relatively new branch of medicine, Psycho-neuroimmunology (PNI), has begun to examine the mind-body connection and its relationship to disease. It is now accepted that stress plays a major role in the manifestation of disease. This mind-body link has been scientifically proven in research laboratories nation wide.
>
> PNI has now established that during stressful situations and negative emotional states, the brain produces neurotransmitters that are toxic to the body's immune system. Conversely, during pleasurable situations and positive emotional states, the brain also produces neurotransmitters which enhance the body's immune system.[8]

The new science and the ancient idea emphasize the existence and active component of a spiritual dimension to life and health. Dr. Richard Gerber, author of *Vibrational Medicine*, suggests that just like oxygen, water, and sugar, the spirit "nourishes our physical form with higher vibrational energies; spirit is at the very heart of sustaining life itself."[9] For him, if medicine does not include the mind and soul in the healing process, it will ultimately fail.

Even Einstein's work contributes to vibrational medicine theory with his famous $E=mc^2$ equation which suggests "that matter and energy are dual expressions of the nature of the universe."[10] We are all energy; bundles of energy manifested into physical forms which exist as "networks of complex energy field."[11]

---

8.   Ibid., 17-18.
9.   Ibid., 18.
10.   Ibid., 18.
11.   Ibid., 19.

So, instead of viewing and treating physical symptoms as the root of health problems, vibrational medicine seeks to treat the energy imbalance, realigning the person or animal energetically by incorporating the mind and soul with the body as equally important components in the healing process. It does not use drugs or any synthetic human creations, but rather taps into universal sources to use pure energy to restore health.

> Dr. Gerber explains, 'This theoretical network, which represents the physical/cellular framework, is organized and nourished by 'subtle' energetic systems which coordinate the life-force with the body. There is a hierarchy of subtle energetic systems that coordinate electro-physiologic hormonal functions, as well as cellular structure within the physical body. It is primarily from these subtle levels that health and illness originate. These unique energy systems are powerfully affected by our emotions and level of spiritual balance as well as by nutritional and environmental factors. These subtle energies influence cellular patterns of growth in both positive and negative directions.'

> By working with the energetic patterns that influence the physical expression of life, vibrational medicine strives to heal illness and bring consciousness to a higher level.[12]

Essentially, vibrational medicine seeks to heal the whole being and takes responsibility for treating problems at their root causes, and not mask the physical symptoms/manifestations with drugs to alter the physical chemistry in our bodies and/or brains, but to actually heal the problem so that it is absolutely resolved and will not return. This is not unlike the 'quest model' Frateroli describes when discussing the differences between and the advantages of the psychotherapeutic psychiatry model compared to the medical psychiatry model.

Fratteroli describes two models in psychiatry, the 'Medical Model' and the 'Psychotherapeutic Model.' The former believes spiritual and psychological problems, with symptoms, are fundamental problems with brain biochemistry and can be fixed by using drugs to change that brain biochemistry back to 'normal' and eliminate symptoms. The Psychotherapeutic Model, on the other hand, holds that drugs have a place, but are not enough to solve the real problem. This model suggests that spiritual crises have psychological sources, they are not just caused by chemical imbalances. Fratteroli says that we need to move psychiatry back to something that addresses problems as truly deep seated issues that need more than a pill for a quick fix to eliminate the symptoms.

---

12. Ibid., 19.

> ... the very heart of the Psychotherapeutic Model ... understands symptoms as meaningful expressions of the self, in marked contrast to the Medical Model., which treats symptoms as dangerous and alien to the persons who have them. The difference between these two attitudes towards symptoms reflects a deeper difference in attitudes towards people. The Psychotherapeutic Model is grounded in the similarity–the common humanity–between physician and patient. The Medical Model is grounded in scientific research, in which the doctor treats the patient as an object of detached observation.[13]

This division in psychiatry is relatively new. The whole profession of psychiatry has changed in the last fifty years. It used to be that someone undergoing psychiatric help was subject to intense, long-term observation by psychiatrists before any conclusive health evaluation was made. That no longer takes place because it costs a lot of money to keep people for such observation (about the same as it costs to keep people in jail). So, instead of deriving treatment plans for patients from close and careful observation, psychiatrists are now listening to the patient describe their symptoms, prescribing them a drug to try for six weeks (which will be changed if no results occur by that time), and making them promise not to kill themselves before sending them home. This is obviously a much less personal or intuitive method of treatment, and precisely what Fratteroli is trying to point out as being an, at least slightly unorthodox practice of psychiatric medicine.

Fratteroli proposes two philosophical models behind the two psychiatric treatment models because he says,

> There is philosophy implicit in everything we do, though it remains, for the most part, outside of our awareness. What looks like a pragmatic choice of the treatment that works best is, at a deeper level, a choice of philosophy. What we think works best depends on what we are trying to accomplish, which in turn depends on what we think is worth accomplishing, which depends ultimately on our all too often unconscious philosophy of life.[14]

These two philosophical models for life can be paired up with the psychiatric models; Fratteroli calls them the Swimming Pool Model and the Quest Model. In the Swimming Pool Model, you just want to get through life and trudge along a daily routine with as few problems as possible. In this view psychological problems slow you down in life and "falling down is bad". The Quest Model, on the

---

13.   Elio Fratteroli, *Healing the Soul in the Age of the Brain*, (Library of America, 2001), 107.
14.   Ibid., 107-108.

other hand, says it is okay to have problems in life, in fact it embraces them. In this view "falling down is good". Symptoms of psychological problems are good as they can be used to help you grow as a person, get to know and understand yourself and your view of life to get closer to your ultimate goals and overcome the psychological problem.

The Medical Model compliments the Swimming Pool Model as it typically just relies on drug prescriptions to help patients get through their problems by masking symptoms so they can "keep on swimming with their head down." The Psychotherapeutic Model compliments the Quest Model more as it looks at the problems we encounter in life and views them as things that can be talked out and worked through to better understand ourselves and thus enjoy life.

Fratteroli suggests that the Psychotherapeutic and Quest models are preferable to the Medical and Swimming Pool models for a couple of reasons. For one, many religions encourage people to have spiritual experiences and in fact are designed to give individuals these types of experiences. If psychiatrists from the Medical Model are prescribing medications to eliminate these "symptoms" to "fix" people there is a certain discrepancy that poses a problem for the individual. The Medical Model identifies symptoms by asking questions from standardized questionnaires. This makes people lose their identity as they are given a code and a drug to neutralize their behavior, thoughts, and/or emotions. If you only mask the symptoms chemically through medication, the cause of the problem will probably still remain and recur until it is solved from the root. The Psychotherapeutic Model might prescribe drugs for some short-term relief, but it is always coupled with a long-term therapy plan in which patients talk to a professional about their "symptoms" to try and find the root cause of the problem to be worked though and solved completely.

If someone has repeat problem behavior stemming from some psychological trauma, and wants to stop it, the Medical Model would give them a drug to remove the symptoms. The Psychotherapeutic Model gets at and resolves underlying problems and then the symptoms go away on their own, usually permanently. The point of the "quest" is to ultimately help you "get better" and get to a higher level in life. 'Falling down' is good because getting over a problem helps you learn and move forward in life, not just drudge along with masked symptoms. People need to view things in a more positive context. Symptoms shouldn't be seen as problems but as tools that can be used to help us develop as people. If you simply take drugs to mask symptoms you can't learn anything about the problems to apply to your life to get you out of that 'rut' you feel stuck in sometimes.

When asked, more than 50% of people identify their problems as having a spiritual dimension, but they are treated by doctors/psychiatrists who have no training or consideration at all of this element, some in fact feel that belief in such a dimension of a problem *is* the problem that needs to be fixed with medication. Essential elements of some religions are in fact to engage in spiritual practices designed to invoke in people religious experiences. So, while religions encourage this behavior it is viewed as actions and symptoms that need to be "fixed" by the Medical Model of psychiatry. This is a fundamental problem.

Both Reiki and Bach Flower Essences are forms of vibrational medicine which share similar philosophies to the Quest and Psychotherapeutic models. They are non-invasive therapies that use pure energy in two different ways to heal. Interestingly, they originated in two very different parts of the world, and at different periods in time. While Reiki is much older, Dr. Edward Bach is today considered the father of Vibrational Medicine, so let's explore his work first.

Bach Flower Essences

"Bach Flower Essences" is the common name for a set of 38 vibrational medicine flower essences that Dr. Edward Bach discovered in the 1920's and 1930's. These are a type of energy healing that utilize the energy or essence of a number of different flowers to heal primarily emotional upsets. Dr. Bach saw health as existing on an emotional and spiritual level as well as a physical level, and sought to heal them all through simplicity with what he viewed as gifts from nature. The essences are not cures for broken bones or the common flu, they target the imbalances in our emotional and spiritual energies and thereby directly promote improved physical health as well according to Dr. Bach's theories. They, like Frateroli's Quest Model, and the psychotherapeutic psychiatric model, view the problems and upsets of life as stepping stones to a greater existence. Our problems, according to these views are not mere annoyances that we have to suppress in life, but they are building blocks or clues that can teach us about ourselves and can be used as lessons to improve our futures.

> Dr. Bach's new system was based on his perception that disease was a reflection of misalignment between the personality and the soul ... [His] development of his flower remedies, currently known around the world as the Bach Flower Essences, is now viewed as the origin of vibrational medicines. These subtle vibrational energies contained within the flower essences catalyze the realignment of an individual's emotional patterns of dysfunction. This reinstates the proper vibrational frequencies necessary for the restoration of health and wellbeing.[15]

To truly discuss the origin of Bach Flower Essences we must first get to know Dr. Bach himself. He lived from 1886-1936 and throughout his life was always fascinated with and awed by nature. He was a perfectionist and loved people, feeling compelled his whole life to help others which made medicine seem a fitting course of study for him. However, prior to beginning medical school Bach did indeed consider a more prominently religious career choice.

> He saw also that little was done for the greater number of their complaints beyond palliation and suppression of symptoms, and he determined to find a way to ease their minds and heal their bodies, for he was still convinced there was a simple method of healing to be found, one which would cure all disease, including those called chronic and incurable.

> It seemed to him that this form of healing perhaps belonged more to the Church than to the medical profession, for Christ, the Great Healer, healed body, mind and soul; and he debated within himself which profession he should enter.

> But neither seemed fully to interpret his ideals ... [16]

Still, he decided the best route for him to pursue his personal goals and intuitions was to study medicine, to learn about all the current methods of curing patients, and then to maintain the ability to think critically and ask the questions others were afraid to, or trained not to, about the limitations of modern medicine. He began his studies in 1906 at Birmingham University, and then completed his training in London at University College Hospital in 1912, though he continued his studies to obtain post degrees and a Diploma of Public Health by 1914. Throughout his years as a physician, he practiced medicine in different hospitals, in private practice in his own office on Harley Street in London, and in a number of different positions.

> His ideal of a simple way to heal all disease persisted, and as he grew older it became a conviction and the activating force behind his whole life's work, for throughout the years he practiced as a pathologist, bacteriologist and homeopath his one aim was to find pure remedies, a simple form of treatment to replace the complicated scientific means which gave no certainty of cure.[17]

---

15. Hasnas, *The Essence of Bach Flowers*, 20-21.
16. Nora Weeks, *The Medical Discoveries of Edward Bach Physician*, (United Kingdom: Vermillion, 2004), 13.
17. Ibid., 11.

He believed it incredibly important to include the individual in their treatment, and was completely dissatisfied with the idea that good medicine was to be objective, and treat the body, the symptoms without much, if any consideration of the person they were attached to. So, throughout his career Dr. Bach spent hours studying his patients, and people in general. He wanted to find a method of healing that was permanent, and did not simply mask symptoms, or provide a temporary cure, and he wanted to be able to heal with a gentle, rather than an invasive method. "To him, the true study of disease lay in watching every patient, observing the way in which each one was affected by his complaint, and seeing how these different reactions influenced the course, severity and duration of the disease."[18]

Bach maintained his ability to think critically throughout his life, and would only typically use widely accepted theories after he proved them to himself.[19] He was frustrated with medicine that treated the disease instead of the person, and believed that neglecting the contribution of the person inside the body to its state of health, and attributing both disease and cure to strictly physiological entities was to oversimplify and generalize bodies. Through his observations of patients, he witnessed that the same treatments did not have the same effects on different patients, with the same complaints. This remains true of today's modern medicine—we are only given an educated estimate of what the effects of treatments will be based on how most people respond to treatments. This was both unacceptable and unnecessary to Dr. Bach.

Over time he concluded from his observations that while people with the same physical problems did not always respond the same to the same treatments, people with similar personalities and different problems *did* often respond the same to the same treatments. He recognized that identical procedures or treatments did not work the same in different patients, and success varied with most medical treatments. This suggested to him that personalities are indeed important in health and the treatment of illnesses. It also indicates that illness and health reflect multidimensional existences, and are not just physical problems, but do indeed have emotional and perhaps spiritual components as well.

> … he began to question the current medical practice of standard treatments for specific diseases. Eventually, he began to also notice that patients with similar personality would often respond to the same treatment regardless of their

18.   Ibid., 16.
19.   Ibid., 17.

particular disease. Those individuals with different personalities needed other medical attention although they experienced the same disease.

> In this way Dr. Bach came to understand that it was the personality of an individual that was more important than the body in regard to the treatment of disease. This remarkable insight–treat the individual, not the disease–became the cornerstone of the new system of medicine that he would develop some 20 years later.[20]

Despite what critics might say about Dr. Bach's methods of following his own intuition and searching for simple answers being unorthodox, he is one of the few scientists capable of thinking critically enough to see the flaws in the established, accepted, standardized system of modern medicine. His decision to not blindly accept scientific 'objective' tradition allowed him to recognize that standardized treatments ultimately do not work for everyone and are subsequently ineffective. This is a problem that persists today in Western medicine, but most physicians are either taught or decide to accept such limits to the medicine they use. We still treat cancer patients with chemicals and invasive, traumatic procedures that only have an estimated percentile rating of success which isn't often accurate. This common practice that continues today, of medicine focused on symptoms and results, rather than causes was what Dr. Bach refused to accept. Just like Frateroli suggested was problematic with the "Swimming pool" and medical model of psychiatric treatment, Dr. Bach believed that in providing health treatments which mask the outcome of the cause without treating the source of the problem was unsatisfactory, and ultimately a failed attempt at healing.

> Surprisingly, Dr. Bach considered disease itself to be beneficial. Illness is a wake-up call from our soul, which reminds us that we are out of alignment with our life's purpose. Disease only comes to us as a signal to nudge us back on track, to be true to ourselves and the higher purpose for which we were born.[21]

Dr. Bach continued to investigate personality and treatment similarities in patients and as a Bacteriologist at University College Hospital, "discovered that certain intestinal germs, which up to then had been considered of little or no importance, were closely connected with chronic disease and its cure."[22] He

---

20. Hasnas, *The Essence of Bach Flowers*, 22-23
21. Hasnas, *The Essence of Bach Flowers*, 25.
22. Weeks, *Medical Discoveries*, 20.

found that such germs existed in everyone, but were disproportionately greater in those with ill health. After much study he was able to create a vaccine from these germs that could be injected and help cure the ill person. Though he was not pleased with having to use the method of injection to administer his vaccine, Dr. Bach was quite happy to find that the overall effect was greater and reactions less when vaccines were administered at irregular intervals, only when the patient seemed to need it and not by strict or regulated schedule. His vaccines were used unofficially "to inoculate the troops in certain home camps" during the influenza epidemic in 1918, and seem to have decreased the death-rate as compared to other camps.[23] His work with intestinal toxaemia was "published in medical journals and are recorded in the Proceedings of the Royal Society of Medicine for the year 1920".[24]

Eventually Dr. Bach left his post with the medical industry and became increasingly intrigued and impressed by Homeopathic medicines he learned about. Though originally quite skeptical about this field of healing, Dr. Bach quickly changed his tune about Homeopathy after reading *Organon* by Hahnemann, who is known as the founder of homeopathy. The book reflected much of his own ideals and scientific discoveries though it was written many years prior. "The cures which Hahnemann had obtained were doubly marvelous to Edward Bach's mind in that he had used not germs, the products of disease, but remedies culled mainly from Nature, Her plants and herbs and mosses."[25] Bach studied more of Hahnemann's work and found that instead of having to use his injectable vaccines he could prepare the medicines without germs, but from plants through the homeopathic method and have patients take them orally with the same results. He was moving closer to his goal of finding a simple and non-invasive method of healing.

Ultimately there were seven bacterial "nosodes" or oral vaccines which Bach was determined to replace with some plant or herb. This work began in 1928 for Bach, where he followed his intuition to find what he sought and has become so well known for. One night while at a banquet dinner, Bach countered his boredom by watching the people at the dinner.

> ... suddenly he realized that the whole of humanity consisted of a number of definite groups of types; that every individual in that large hall belonged to one or other of these groups ... how they ate their food, how they smiled and

---

23.   Weeks, *Medical Discoveries*, 23.
24.   Weeks, *Medical Discoveries*, 24.
25.   Weeks, *Medical Discoveries*, 26.

moved their hands and heads, the attitudes of their bodies, the expressions on their faces and … the tone of voice they used. So close was the resemblance between certain people that they might have belonged to the same family, although there was no blood relation.[26]

He had distilled a number of groups and began to wonder how this observation would relate to his study of disease and treatments. "Then came the inspiration that the individuals of each group would *not* suffer from the same kinds of diseases, but that all those in any one group would react in the same or nearly the same manner to any type of illness."[27] This inspiration led him to observe his patients even more closely from then on and he became able to successfully prescribe remedies for patients based on his observations of their personalities alone.

Further intuitions led Bach into the country and to find a series of plants which he would prepare and prescribe for patients according to their personality which he observed to have "immediate and remarkable results."[28] He became so excited with his newest discoveries in these plants that he made the decision to leave his lucrative practice in pursuit of this new medicine.

At last he told his friends that he was about to give up his work in London and devote himself to the task of finding world-types and searching for the further remedies which would heal these types and, by so doing, heal all the diseases from which they might suffer.[29]

Bach had, in 1917 suffered a severe hemorrhage and became unconscious, undergoing a risky surgery through which many doubted he would survive. He did, obviously come through the surgery, but was told he had only about three months to live by his surgeons. Despite all this, Bach felt as though his life's work had yet to be complete so he set to work in a hurry and his health grew stronger with time. He attributes his increased health to the fact that he was pursuing a goal that inspired his higher self and created a peace and vibrational balance between his personality and his soul, resonating to improve his physical health subsequently. He said in an address to the British Homeopathic Society on November 1, 1928 titled "The Rediscovery of Psora," "Science is tending to show that life is harmony–a state of being in tune–and that disease is discord or a

---

26. Weeks, *Medical Discoveries*, 40.
27. Weeks, *Medical Discoveries*, 40.
28. Weeks, *Medical Discoveries*, 41.
29. Weeks, *Medical Discoveries*, 42.

condition when a part of the whole is not vibrating in unison." Bach lived much longer than anyone thought he would, and died only shortly after declaring his Flower Essence work complete.

The 38 Bach Flower Essences

Over several years Dr. Bach discovered intuitively 38 vibrational essences to heal problems of a spiritual and emotional nature which manifestations are observed in personalities. These essences can be used individually or mixed in any combination with one another such that Dr. Bach believes they can respond to all possible negative mental states, which is why he declared his work complete when he did; he saw no need for any others and his intuition told him his work was complete. These remedies are not intended to cure physical ailments, but rather prevent their manifestation by establishing peace and balance in our spiritual and emotional dimensions. "… each one of them is aimed at a different state of mind or emotion. They do not treat physical illness directly, but by restoring harmony to the mind they allow the body's natural defenses to work more easily."[30]

Bach broke down the essences to seven groups, for Fear, Uncertainty, Insufficient Interest in Present Circumstances, Loneliness, Oversensitivity to Influences and Ideas, Despondency or Despair, and Over-care for Welfare of Others. Interestingly, the first twelve he found have been determined to correlate with Astrological, or Zodiac signs for people's 'types'. The following is a chart set out by Astrologer Rachelle Hasnas, M.S.W. in *The Essence of Bach Flowers* indicating the original, or first twelve states of mind Bach found with his first twelve essences, the flower type essence that correlates to it, and the zodiac sign that relates to the former two.

State of Mind	Type Essence	Natal Moon Sign
1. Impatience	Impatience	Aries
2. Doubt/Discouragement	Gentian	Taurus
3. Self-distrust	Cerato	Gemini
4. Indifference/Boredom	Clematis	Cancer
5. Over-enthusiasm	Vervain	Leo
6. Weakness	Centaury	Virgo

---

30. Stefan Ball, *The Bach Remedies Workbook: A study Course in the Bach Flower Remedies*, (London: Vermilion, 2005), 20.

7.	Indecision	Scleranthus	Libra
8.	Over-concern	Chicory	Scorpio
9.	Mental Torture/Worry	Agrimony	Sagittarius
10.	Fear	Mimulus	Capricorn
11.	Pride/Aloofness	Water Violet	Aquarius
12.	Terror	Rock Rose	Pisces

Essences for Fear

In this category there are five essences for different kinds of fear. It is important to note that for all the essences, there is both a positive and negative state, whereby the flower essence helps those suffering from the negative states balance their energy such that they can enjoy the positive state.

Mimulus (Botanical Name: *Mimulus guttatus*) is the remedy for fear of known things, or things that one can name. Death, the dark, the dentist, spiders, crowds, public speaking; these are all examples of what people might be afraid of for which Mimulus can help. The positive potential of Mimulus is a personality with quiet courage in adversity and the pursuit of life without fear.

Rock Rose (*Helianthemum nummularium*) is the remedy for terror or severe fright. This is one of the remedies that is especially good for treating acute problems, such as after an accident or nightmare, etc. "The positive potential of Rock Rose is courage and presence of mind; the person who is calm and self-forgetful in emergencies."[31]

Aspen (*Populus tremula*) is the remedy for fear of unknown, or unidentifiable things. This would be helpful for people with sudden and unprovoked panic or anxiety attacks that they cannot explain. The positive potential of Aspen is a state of inner peace and security where instead of fear one welcomes new experience and adventure.

Cherry Plum (*Prunus cerasifera*) is the remedy for fear of losing self control. This is for times when one feels as if they may 'explode' with emotion, have a violent outburst, or lose control of their behavior. It may also be helpful for situations like post-partum depression. "The positive potential of Cherry Plum is the person who has a calm mind and is able to think and act rationally."[32]

---

31. Bach Shop Direct, "The Remedy Chooser" http://www.bachshop.co.uk/catalog/index.php/cPath/32
32. Ibid.

Red Chestnut (*Aesculus carnea*) is the remedy for fear of something happening to loved ones. This is to help those who stress themselves with worry for friends and family, for their physical well being and emotional problems as well and often will not stop their worries until those of concern are known to be home, or safely in the presence of the worrier. This is a selfless fear, but a stressful one. The positive potential of Red Chestnut is the ability to care for others with compassion but without anxiety and an eagerness to offer help, but not by being forceful or overbearing.

Essences for Uncertainty

Dr. Bach identified six of his remedies to this category.

Cerato (*Ceratostigma willmottiana*) is the remedy for self doubt, or difficulty trusting ones' own decisions. People in need of this remedy typically know what it is they want, but feel compelled to collect advice and opinions from others before making decisions, and often trust this advice from others instead of their own intuitions. The positive potential of Cerato is the ability to trust inner wisdom and intuitions and be confident in decisions.

Scleranthus (*Scleranthus annuus*) is the remedy for indecision. It is for those who constantly second guess their decisions and have difficulty even with minuet ones, like which loaf of bread to buy at the market. These people tend to know or hold end goals, but have difficulty deciding how exactly to obtain them, they often waste time and miss opportunities because of their inability to make decisions easily. "The positive potential of Scleranthus is certainty and decisiveness, with poise and balance in all circumstances. Positive Schleranthus people are able to make quick decisions and act promptly when necessary."[33]

Gentian (*Gentiana amarelle*) is the remedy for discouragement. It is to help those who are easily upset or depressed by identifiable causes, like difficult schoolwork or illness. The positive potential of Gentian assures confidence and optimism in every task that sees one through difficulties and is not overcome with or deterred by doubt.

Gorse (*Ulex europoeus*) is the remedy for despair, pessimism, hopelessness, and the feeling of giving up. It is more severe than Gentian. However, the positive potential of Gorse is a sense of hope in the face of adversity, and cheerful or optimistic feelings about life's difficulties as positive opportunities.

Hornbeam (*Carpinus betulus*) is the remedy for procrastination or the 'Monday morning feeling'. It is for those who have difficulty getting started on tasks,

---

33.   Ibid.

but once they have begun are content to continue. The positive potential of Hornbeam is confidence in one's ability to face and accomplish the work ahead, with clarity and focus.

Wild Oat (*Bromus ramosus*) is the remedy for lack of direction particularly at crossroads in life. It is helpful for those who tend to make decisions easily, but are often dissatisfied with their choices because they do not know what they want as a final goal—it is almost the opposite of Scleranthus. The positive potential of Wild Oat is a clear and defined life picture. They are able to put their talents to effective use and do not quit when bored.

Essences for Insufficient Interest in Present Circumstances

There are seven essences for this group.

Clematis (*Clematis vitalba*) is the remedy for bringing people back to reality when living in daydreams. These dreamers may have elaborate imaginings and dreams in their minds, but never seeks to create them in the real world. These types also tend to keep to themselves and not have much energy, and may seem absent minded. The positive potential of Clematis is an interest in the present, with a sense of purpose, inspiration, and creativity in the world and strong grounding.

Honeysuckle (*Lonicera caprifolium*) is the remedy for those who tend to live in the past and dwell on memories. This is helpful for those who have difficulty recovering from regretful past events, have lost loved ones, or are homesick and have difficulty finding happiness in the present situations. The positive potential of Honeysuckle is the ability to live in the present, and not overwhelmed with nostalgia. The passing of time and aging is welcomed as a positive thing.

Wild Rose (*Rosa canina*) is the remedy for those who seem stuck in their lives. They are typically in an unpleasant situation or illness, but make little or no effort to improve their condition and have resigned to accept this existence. They are often apathetic and not overly unhappy with their state. They are not energetic or ambitious and are missing their potential. The positive potential of Wild Rose has renewed sense of purpose and appreciation for life. One is able to accept responsibility for the situations they find themselves in and actively work to change what is not desirable.

Olive (*Olea europoea*) is the remedy for exhaustion in mind and body. This is for those who have been over worked physically or mentally or emotionally, after too much stress or study, a long or severe illness of their own or a loved one, etc. For those needed the Olive essence life has become less pleasant, burdensome and tiring to the point of tears. The positive potential of Olive is renewed strength and an increased respect for one's limits.

White Chestnut (*Aesculus hippocastanum*) is the remedy for quieting unwanted or repetitive thoughts. This is helpful for people with trouble sleeping because of a busy mind, or obsessively worry, think about, or relive negative events or conversations. The positive potential of White Chestnut is tranquility and a quiet mind and clear head. Stress and worry are exchanged for faith in positive results and ideas for problem solving.

Mustard (*Sinapis arvensis*) is the remedy for depression that develops without known cause but that is difficult to shake. "The positive potential of Mustard is the return of joy, supported by an inner stability and peace which cannot be shaken or destroyed under good circumstances or bad."[34]

Chestnut Bud (*Aesculus hippocastanum*) is the remedy for the inability to learn from experiences. It is for those who continue to make the same mistakes or have the same difficulties in life because they fail to remember the lessons from previous experiences. Examples may be that these sufferers continue to fail the same tests, choose inappropriate partners, make poor business choices, all because their typical response to failure is to dismiss and forget it altogether, thereby losing valuable information with which to base future decisions on. The positive potential of Chestnut Bud is the ability to contemplate and learn from every experience, both personal and observed, and to employ this new knowledge in future experiences to progress in life.

Essences for Loneliness

Water Violet (*Hottonia palustris*) is the remedy for helping to deconstruct the walls independent people can build up around themselves. It is to help these people enjoy the company of others more and seem less snobbish or arrogant. The positive potential of Water Violet is the ability to open up to others, to trust, understand, and empathize with other people while keeping in touch with and benefiting from one's own knowledge and wisdom.

Impatiens (*Impatiens glandulifera*) is the remedy for just what it seems–impatience. This is the remedy for those who are constantly in a hurry and easily frustrated or irritated by others who tend to do things differently or more slowly. The positive potential of Impatiens is the ability to approach tasks with a relaxed attitude, calm mind and not be so easily irritated by slower-paced people.

---

34. Ibid.

Heather (*Calluna vulgaris*) is the remedy for those who seem self centered, or constantly make themselves the center of attention and tend to neglect others' problems. These are very needy, often dramatic people who tend to be draining to their audience. "The positive potential of Heather is the good listener who is generous in helping others, selfless and understanding of other people's problems. Positive Heather people are able to put their own suffering to good use by empathizing with others."[35]

Essences for Over-Sensitivity to Influences and Ideas

Agrimony (*Agrimonia eupatoria*) is the remedy for silent sufferers, or those who hide their problems or discontentment behind a mask of happiness. The positive potential of Agrimony is the ability to accept difficulties in life and express their range of emotions honestly.

Centaury (*Centaurium umbellatum*) is the remedy for those who cannot say 'no'. For those who make every effort to constantly please everyone around them, and possibly be taken advantage of, Centaury can help. The positive potential of Centaury is a personality that is willing and eager to help others, but not to an extent that will overexert themselves emotionally or physically. These people are able to contribute to discussions or debates with confidence, their own perspectives.

Walnut (*Juglans regia*) is the remedy for change and influence by others. It is good for big changes in life, career changes, moving, changing schools for children, getting married, getting divorced, etc. But it is also helpful to aid people in standing their ground when feeling pressured to alter their decisions and neglect their intuitions because of the influence of others advising against it. "The positive potential of Walnut is the ability to move forward and remain steadfast to one's path in life, free of the past and to make necessary changes in life, carrying plans through despite discouragement, objections or ridicule from others. It is the remedy that provides constancy and protection from the influence of others."[36]

Holly (*Ilex aquifolium*) is the remedy for negative feelings like suspicion, revenge, envy, jealousy or hatred. It is for people who can be cruel or violent without cause, and are constantly unhappy without reason. The positive potential of Holly is unrequited generosity and abundant compassion.

---

35.   Ibid.
36.   Ibid.

Essences for Despondency or Despair

<u>Larch</u> (*Larix deciduas*) is the remedy for helping those who lack confidence and feel inferior or incapable. "The positive potential of Larch is expressed in people who are determined, capable, with a realistic sense of self esteem, unworried about failure or success. They are aware of their own potential and work towards achieving it. They are able to take the initiative, to take risks, and refuse to accept the word 'can't'. They use their critical faculties sensibly."[37]

<u>Pine</u> (*Pinus sylvestris*) is the remedy for those who tend to blame themselves and feel guilty for every upset, even those they are not responsible for. The positive potential of Pine is a clearer perspective of oneself, and the ability to accept and reject responsibility for circumstances pragmatically.

<u>Elm</u> (*Ulmus procera*) is the remedy for those who feel as though their responsibilities are overwhelming. It is not that these people are incapable of accomplishing their work, they just feel overwhelmed by the quantity of it and can become tired and intimidated at the thought of it. The positive potential of Elm is a renewed sense of confidence for tasks ahead as well as the ability to see things from a less daunting perspective.

<u>Sweet Chestnut</u> (*Castanea sativa*) is the remedy for those who have lost all hope, and feel trapped or cornered in their life situation. It is different from the Gorse type, because that one should be identified as the remedy for one who has chosen to give up, or simply lost their faith whereas the Sweet Chestnut type is one who has been subjected to their state by outside circumstances and are incapable of changing them. "The positive potential of Sweet Chestnut is liberation from despair and despondency. Though external circumstances may not have changed, they can now be faced with optimism and peace of mind. This may be aided by the discovery or recovery of faith in a higher power and a sense of inner support."[38]

<u>Star of Bethlehem</u> (*Ornithogalum umbetelatum*) is the remedy for shock or grief. It is particularly useful for traumatic situations, emotional and physical, but it is also effective at healing imbalances from past traumas, even years previous to the treatment. The positive potential of Star of Bethlehem is to help one heal from any traumatic suffering ever experienced.

<u>Willow</u> (*Salix vitellina*) is the remedy for those who engage in self-pity and who defer responsibility onto others. These types are sulky, and displeased by successes of others, and never satisfied with their own situations. The positive

---

37. Ibid.
38. Ibid.

potential of Willow is the ability for forgiveness and release of experienced negativity and sense of victimization.

Oak (*Quercus robur*) is the remedy for those who persist in their efforts no matter how tired they become. Oak is to help these types remember to rest, and permit themselves a break when they are stressed but more work remains. The positive potential of Oak is the ability to recognize and respect one's own limits and to nurture one's self for increased endurance and strength in the face of adversity.

Crab Apple (*Malus sylvestris*) is the remedy for cleansing, and helping those who feel negatively about parts or all of their appearance, or their homes or environment. This remedy can also be applied externally for help to cleanse impurities or imperfections in the skin.

Remedies for Over-Care for the Welfare of Others

Chicory (*Cichorium intybus*) is the remedy for those who are overly attached to or possessive of loved ones, for parents or children who have separation anxieties and for those who desperately want to be close to the ones they care about. The overprotective parent, or possessive child would benefit from this remedy well. "The positive potential of Chicory is seen in people who are able to care for others unselfishly, offering genuine maternal love. They give without expecting anything back and allow their loved ones to be themselves and live their own lives. Feeling fulfilled and self-assured, they no longer need other people's assurance that they are worthy of love. They are warm, kind, concerned for others and sensitive to other people's needs."[39]

Vervain (*Verbena officinalis*) is the remedy for over enthusiasm for a cause, and for those who often strive to convert others to adopt opinions or lifestyles. Vervain is for strong willed, over-achievers who put their hearts into their work and are confident and steadfast in their beliefs. The positive potential of Vervain is the ability to posses and share strong opinions without forcing them on others, and also tolerate different and even opposite opinions.

Vine (*Vitis vinifera*) is the remedy for those who are forceful and demanding leaders, or tyrants. It is a more severe type than Vervain, not interested in convincing others to adopt or share their view, but aggressively demand this conformity. "The positive potential of Vine is determination without domination. Positive Vine people see the good in others and encourage and guide without controlling them. They make wise leaders, teachers, bosses or parents. They use

---

39. Ibid.

their gifts to help others to know themselves and find their own path in life. They inspire others with their unshakeable confidence and certainty." [40]

Beech (*Fagus sylvatica*) is the remedy for those who are intolerant of others, feel superior and are intensely judgmental. This is the type who refuses to accept when they are wrong. The positive potential of Beech is the ability to see the good, or potential good in everyone and express tolerance for any flaws or blemishes in their character.

Rock Water (*Aqua petra*–this is the only remedy not made from a flowering tree or plant, but from a spring in Whales) is the remedy for perfectionists who would not tell someone to change their ways, but instead attempts to set an influential example with their own actions. They are strict and controlling, but of themselves instead of others. They tend to deny themselves simple pleasures and set high standards for themselves but are rarely satisfied with their own efforts. The positive potential of Rock Water is an ability to give up or modify their ideals if/when presented with a 'truer truth'.

Rescue Remedy

Dr. Bach created just one standard mix of these remedies which he called 'Rescue Remedy' to use for emergencies, but any combination of the 38 remedies can be custom mixed for the individual needs of patients, just as Dr. Bach thought treatment should exist–based on the patient, not the disease. In Rescue Remedy however, there is Star of Bethlehem, Rock Rose, Clematis, Impatiens and Cherry Plum essences. He decided to make this mix so that it would be ready and available in times of emergency, for accidents or dramatic situations when a mix is needed suddenly. It is also an excellent mix for feelings of distress from arguments, for exam nerves, needles or doctor's appointments, etc.

Methods of Preparation & How it Works

Above are the 38 individual essences and 1 ready-mixed remedy discovered and created by Dr. Bach. But how exactly do the essences work, and how are they made? Essentially the essences 'work' through energy and there are two different methods Bach used to collect the essences of the flowers, the Sun Method and the Boiling Method.

The basic premise of Bach's theory with his Flower essences was not that they would help people to become new or different people, but rather more 'themselves'.

---

40.   Ibid.

Dr Bach believed that we are all here on earth to learn from who we are. Our time on the planet is an opportunity to discover our strengths and to work on our weaknesses. Doing this does not mean becoming someone else; instead, it means working to find out who we really are. It means finding the richness in being ourselves, rather than trying to be someone else.[41]

For Bach, we are all spiritual beings, and our existence can be broken down to two halves: a soul, and a personality. The soul is in his theory the spiritual and immortal aspect of ourselves which has a higher purpose or goal for us to reach in our life. The personality is the earthly manifestation and mental 'stuff' which combined with the soul makes the whole person. While the soul is considered perfect by Bach, the personality has limitations such that it can be tempted and distracted from outside influences that can bump it out of alignment from the goals and higher purpose of the soul. When such disruption occurs in the alignment of our whole person, the vibrations of our emotional, spiritual, and physical energies are unbalanced and sickness and disease can manifest out of this 'disease' in our whole existence. Bach also believed that we can become out of balance with the vibrational unity of the universe when we harm or are negative to others which is also an opportunity for disease or illness to take hold.

The Bach Flower Essences work to re-balance us from any and all of the potential negative states our lives may lead us to. When we feel fear, uncertainty, despair or any of the seven groups Bach identified, we might be approaching a situation that could upset our energy alignment. The remedies, when taken correctly, supply the corresponding vibrational energy to either re-balance or prevent a disruption in our energy balance altogether.

The Bach Flower Essences are often used with the analogy of peeling an onion, whereas our energetic imbalances are believed to establish layers with time, where different essences are needed over time, to treat different negative emotions that may have stacked up before the initial imbalance is revealed. "This means that the action of the remedies is *restorative*, in that they work to bring us back to who we were when things began to go wrong."[42] That said, the remedies do not complete our spiritual growth or evolution for us, by changing who we are, they merely help us to find the opposite, positive state of the negative state or states we are living in as a result of energy imbalances.

---

41. Stefan Ball, *Thorsons Principles of Bach Flower Remedies*, (London: Thorsons, 1999), 29.

42. Ball, *Principles*, 36.

The science behind how energy works in our bodies is still quite young and there was very little of it in Bach's time. As was discussed earlier, recent science (namely Psycho-neuroimmunology) has indicated how stress and negative emotional states physically create toxins to our immune system and positive emotional states enhance it.[43] We can suspect that the vibrational energy from each of the essences Bach discovered have similar effects as positive emotional states on our brain and immune system, neutralizing the harmful effects of the negative states. However, this has not been proven by any research collected for this book.

Bach suggested that those who would benefit most from this system he discovered would be the ones who kept it free from science. This was in part because he did not require science to find the essences, nor did he use science to determine whether or not they worked. He observed the results without feeling the need to explain in detail or precision how it worked physiologically. More importantly, Bach's ultimate goal was to discover a method of healing that was simple and non-invasive, and that could be used and understood by everyone, not just those who had advanced education. "The remedies do not work in the same way that orthodox drugs work, by dampening down symptoms. Instead they work by enhancing our existing positive qualities. The negative state isn't suppressed, but removed by an increase in the corresponding positive quality."[44] Bach's message was clear: "theories as to the way the remedies work do not help us to use them effectively."[45]

The two methods of harvesting the essences from the flowers are also simple and both involve heat and water. Bach became incredibly sensitive to the energy of plants in the last decade of his life, such that he was noted for being "able to feel the effects of a flower simply by holding it in his hands: some would bring calm and strength, while others would cause nausea and other physical reactions."[46] This sensitivity coupled with his intuition led him to discover the transfer of essence-energy from flowers into sun-warmed dew drops in the summer heat. This natural preparation delighted Bach, but it seemed impractical to have to collect sun-warmed dew drops off flower petals to fill stock bottles of the essences, so he attempted a similar technique which proved to be equally effective and much more efficient. He placed the flowers in a bowl of water and set it in the sun for a few hours to transfer the energy potency from the flowers to the water. This process is called "the Sun Method" and is still used today.

---

43.   Hasnas, *The Essence of Bach Flowers*, 17.
44.   Ball, *Principles*, xiii.
45.   Ball, *Principles*, 37.
46.   Ball, *Principles*, 7.

The other method is "the Boiling Method" which Bach discovered again through intuitive suggestion, to prepare early spring blossoms, like Cherry Plum twigs in March, when the sun proved to be not quite warm enough for the process. So, Bach tried boiling the flowers he was drawn to in the spring and after letting the water cool, removed the liquid to test as the remedy. He found that it worked, and so this method also persists in the preparation of about half of Bach's Essences today.

Critiques of Bach's Flower Essences

The water from both the Sun and Boiling methods has an equal portion of Brandy mixed with it to preserve the water and these mixes are considered the mother tinctures, from which custom mixes can be made. The individual essences and Rescue Remedy can be purchased in 10 or 20 ml bottles, and the custom mixes are to be prepared in 30 ml bottles. One might suspect the alcohol content in these mixes to be high, but the proper dosage from a stock bottle of any individual essence or rescue remedy is just two drops either on the tongue or pulse points, or preferably in a glass of water (4 drop for rescue remedy because it is a mix itself). So, it is unlikely any problems should arise from the alcohol content of 2 half drops of Brandy matched with energized spring or mineral water. On top of that, a custom mix can be made in the 30 ml dropper bottle with pure spring water and just two drops of each of the selected essences. Four drops of this mix, four times per day is the proper treatment dosage according to Dr. Bach. Again, the alcohol content is even less–such that the only plausible problem with the alcohol content of these might be a religious offense to alcohol itself, not a health hazard.

Consider that a 'shot' of alcohol measures approximately 44ml. Less than half of that amount is the largest bottle Bach Flower Essences are sold in, and what's more, only a maximum of half the content of the bottle is alcohol, the rest is water. So, one who suggests the alcohol content of these essences is dangerous must also believe that one eighth to one quarter of a shot of alcohol is dangerous to our health. Even so, that is suggesting that the whole bottle be consumed at once, when in fact it is intended to be consumed 2 drops at a time. I would argue that such a claim to the 'danger' of these products be both irrational and ridiculous. However, this is the main critique against Bach Flower Essences, second to the suggestion that they are merely placebos.

Are Bach Flower Essences Just Placebos?

Lynn McCutcheon's article "Bach Flower Remedies: Time to Stop Smelling the Flowers?" in the 1995 July/August issue of Skeptical Inquirer makes a number of criticisms against Dr. Bach and his Flower Essences to which I will address only a few, for the rest are weak or altogether insignificant. She is one who argues that the alcohol content in the bottles is great enough to be dangerous or harmful. But she also suggests matter-of-factly that in order for anything to have the potential to heal, it must also have equal potential to harm.

> For example, what if a person who is nearly without fear ingests mimulus? Couldn't she become so fearless that she might attempt to stop an armed robbery? What about the person who already harbors few regrets? If he takes honeysuckle, which supposedly reduces regretful feelings, might he not increase the risk of developing into a full-fledged psychopath?[47]

First of all, Honeysuckle does not remove regretful feelings, it helps those who may have regrets and are stuck dwelling on the past, or the 'good old days' to focus on and live more in the present. But second, this is completely the wrong understanding of how energy therapies work. They do not target bodily or physiological ailments, nor is their healing directed or manifested in the body itself. They do not work at all the same as an antibiotic or cough medicine. Instead of 'fixing' a problem by battling or killing the 'bad cells/germs' as the popular analogy of Western medicine goes, vibrational and energy medicine does not 'destroy' or 'fight' anything, they supply a greater quantity of the positive opposite to the negative state such that it neutralizes the imbalance, realigning the whole being. The energy does not ever change a person. It helps them stabilize their energy in the positive center of potential mind states, and does not lead them to either extreme end of the continuum.

> The action of the remedies is *restorative*, in that they work to bring us back to who we were when things began to go wrong ... people sometimes interpret the action of the remedies in a different way, and see them not as restorative but as *aspirational*–in other words, actually carrying out the growth and evolution for us, helping us to turn into something else. To see how false this idea is we only have to look at what happens when people take remedies. A shy, timid person taking the correct remedy will regain that natural quiet courage that

---

47. Lynn McCutcheon, "Bach Flower Remedies: Time to Stop Smelling the Flowers?" *Skeptical Inquirer* (July/August 1995): 2 of 4.

will allow him to face up to things instead of running from them, but he will not turn into a flamboyant daredevil. Indeed, if a person were to take some potion to change his nature in this way he would only be making himself even further out of balance in a different direction.... balance itself is not to be found at the extremes of our ups and downs. Instead it lies at the midpoint of the seesaw, where we are who we are.[48]

To suggest that Flower Essences are necessarily capable of harm is to consider them on the same level and category as biological medicines when in fact they are something altogether different, and treat our personality and emotion, not our body or even brain chemistry. They are not intended or believed to treat or remove symptoms, they are intended to cure emotional and spiritual imbalances and as a result may improve our physical health or balance in our brain chemistry.

Perhaps the most common and predictable critique of Bach's Flower Essences is that they are merely placebos. "Any favorable results stemming from the use of the Bach Flower Remedies are probably the result of nothing more than a placebo effect."[49] There have been a couple of randomized, double-blind tests completed at different universities in the US and UK to determine whether or not different Bach Flower Essences are effective at relieving anxiety or had the same effect as a placebo. All of these tests which concluded no difference in efficacy between the placebo and Rescue Remedy noted difficulty in collecting data from enough participants to be considered a viable study, often testing exam stress on healthy students, most of whom dropped out of the experiment prior to completion. There has been much dispute between academics over the validity of these experiments and their results as is well documented by the Bach Flower Research Program—http://www.edwardbach.org/edwardbach.htm.

I think it important to include consideration for what Bach's students say in response to the placebo accusation. They suggest that to claim the results occurred merely because the patient believed they would be applies to all medical therapies. Stephan Ball says, "a placebo effect is the power of positive thinking. If you think something is good for you then you will feel better. When you have a headache and take an aspirin part of the effect of the aspirin is to build up your confidence that the headache will go."[50] He continues,

---

48. Ball, *Principles*, 36-37.
49. McCutcheon, "Bach Flower Remedies," 3 of 4.
50. Ball, *Principles*, 42.

The strength of the placebo effect can be demonstrated by looking at its opposite—the *nocebo* effect. The nocebo effect is the power of negative thinking. It takes place when a drug that we know works is given to someone who believes either that the drug does not work, or that it is only a dummy drug.... Skeptics who approach the remedies firmly convinced that they do not work are more likely than others to have their prejudices confirmed.... There is of course more to orthodox medicine than belief, and again the same is true of the remedies. This is shown by the fact that they work on people who do not believe in them ... and people who have been given the remedies without their knowledge have also benefited ... Furthermore the remedies have been shown to be effective with animals and plants, and with very young babies ... It cannot easily be shown that animals and babies respond to suggestion, so the conclusion must be that they are potent in their own right, over and above the placebo effect that they share with all therapies.[51]

The last bit of the above quote is of particular relevance. The Bach Flower Essences work for animals of all kinds, shapes and sizes. This fact negates the criticisms that it is the people who seek these remedies and try the hardest to get well, find the greatest results as McCutcheon flaunts. That trend simply supports the theory on the power of positive thinking and intention. But non-human animals and infants cannot lie, and cannot expect that a remedy given to them secretly by their person, caretaker, or parent will help them emotionally. The results we observe from them must then be considered pure and true, though we must remain cautious that our personal unconscious biases are not influencing our observations, but this can be checked by asking others (preferably unaware of the treatments) for their observations to confirm or dispel our own.

Reiki

Reiki (pronounced Ray-key) is another, similar but also quite different form of vibrational therapy. First of all it is not something that is ingested or applied topically, and it does not come in a tangible medium, but it is another form of healing energy. Reiki is of Japanese origin and can be translated in two parts. The Japanese 'Rei' generally means 'universal' but can carry other meanings as well, notably 'higher knowledge' or 'spiritual consciousness'. The 'Ki' means the same as the Chinese 'Chi' or 'life energy'. "It is also known as the vital life force or the universal life force. This is the non-physical energy that animates all living things. As long as something is alive, it has life energy circulating through it and surrounding it; when it dies, the life energy departs."[52]

---

51. Ball, *Principles*, 42-43.

The healing philosophy with reiki is one that shares similarities again with Bach and Frateroli's Quest model. The idea is that we are more than physical, biological beings and our physical health is affected by the other components of our existence, our mental and spiritual selves. Rand explains that, "If your life energy is low, or if there is a restriction in its flow, you are more vulnerable to illness. When it is high, and flowing freely, you are less likely to get sick. Life energy plays an important role in everything we do. It animates the body and has higher levels of expression. Ki is also the primary energy of our emotions, thoughts and spiritual life."[53] But Reiki as a healing therapy does not come from plants, nor does it come from ourselves despite the fact that Ki is part of it. Reiki comes from a greater source–God, Allah, the Universe, whatever one chooses to believe–and it has its own wisdom, such that it always works for the highest good of all involved. Reiki cannot be used to harm, but its power to reduce stress, promote relaxation and healing are intense. "Reiki can be defined as spiritually guided life energy."[54]

The practice of Reiki can occur in a couple of different forms. Though I do not fully understand the 'how' yet with my own training, I have witnessed the effects of Reiki sent from a distance, and know that it can be sent to the future and the past as well. These may seem far fetched, but really, the concept of time is a human construction, so why should we believe it to limit the capacity for universal energy to work? However, the most common and understandable form of Reiki can be described as a laying on of hands, which is an ancient technique that is also simple enough to be learned by anyone. I am well aware, however, at the significant level of difficulty many people have accepting this type of practice as legitimate healing therapy, so I will elaborate. Dr. Mikao Usui is said to have rediscovered this form of healing in the early 1900's and a growing number of Reiki students and practitioners today can all be traced back to him through Master-Teacher/Student lineages. This does not answer many questions yet, so how is Reiki taught or learned, and what exactly does the laying on of hands healing entail?

There are three levels or degrees in Reiki, one, two and three. The third level is the Master level, and masters are able to 'attune' students to the different levels. An attunement process is the basis for level advancement, but studying Reiki is done by practicing it through administrations of treatments to oneself and others.

52. William Lee Rand, *Reiki: The Healing Touch. First and Second Degree Manual*, JRT & Hayashi Healing Guide Ed. (Michigan: Vision Publications, 2000), 2.

53. Ibid., 2.

54. Ibid., 3.

During an attunement process a student is being made open to the universal energy, such that they may be a vessel for it to flow through to give an energy treatment.

> Reiki is not taught in the way other healing techniques are taught. The ability is transferred to the student by the Reiki Master during an attunement process. During the attunement, the Rei or God-Consciousness makes adjustments in the student's chakras and energy pathways to accommodate the ability to channel Reiki and then links the student to the source of Reiki. These changes are unique for each person. The attunement energies are channeled into the student through the Reiki Master....
>
> The Reiki attunement is a powerful spiritual experience for most people.... Once you have received a Reiki attunement, you will have Reiki for the remainder of your life. It does not wear off and you can never lose it.[55]

Following the attunement process is a 21 day cleanse, where a self treatment is given daily, and the body and mind release toxins and feelings that do not serve the highest good, and habits or beliefs that are no longer useful. It is a complete self cleanse that works for your mind, body and soul and harmonizes the three. It is a period of adjustment and change, but it is also a period of personal growth and spiritual evolution that is intensely refreshing and ultimately peaceful.

Once the cleanse period is complete students must give a Reiki treatment to someone in order to complete their first degree training. This is assisted by instructions from the Reiki Master, or Sensei. The hand positions for self treatments vary some from the treatments given to others; the former is done with standing and seated positions, while the latter is typically given to a client lying on a Reiki or massage table to maximize relaxation. Prior to each Reiki treatment the practitioner must ask the energy to flow through them for the highest good of whoever is being treated. The treatment begins with a series of 4 positions around the head, followed by 4 positions over the torso, one under the back and over and under each knee, and then 4 positions on the feet. These positions however, are just guides and students are encouraged to follow their intuitions about where to position their hands to best suit the energy flow of the treatment. Such intuitions may come in a variety of ways, the practitioner may feel in their own body where a pain or tension exists in the client, or they may feel a difference in the flow of energy in their hands over a particular area. Clients themselves may also experience a movement of energy or different sensations during the reiki treatment. It is

---

55.   Ibid., 4-5.

quite common that a specific pain they were suffering from will move to a different location in their body. When this occurs the Reiki practitioner is generally encouraged to maintain whatever position they had been in when it began to move, they often do not 'follow' or 'chase' the pain as it is misaligned energy that is trying to 'escape'.

There are a number of different colours and sensations that Reiki energy transmits. For example, the different chakras have different corresponding colours, but also during treatments people tend to relax and close their eyes and often comment on being able to see different colours that tend to change when the practitioner changes hand positions. Both the practitioner and the client may experience a wide variety of sensations through the treatment too. I have personally experienced cool, even breeze-like sensations, varying degrees of heat, popping, pulsing and buzzing in different intensities. It is a bit surreal at first, but very exciting.

The basic principles of Reiki encourage humility and are summed up nicely in the following mantra:

Just for today ... Do not worry.
Just for today ... Do not anger.
Honour your parents, teachers and elders.
Earn your living honestly.
Show gratitude to everything.

Similar to the Bach Flower Essence ideology, the practice of Reiki holds that it is through positive thoughts and states that we can increase our Ki, and with negative ones we can interrupt and decrease its flow within us. The power of intension and expectation is significant in the practice of Reiki, such that if it is not with positive intentions a practitioner attempts to send Reiki energy, it simply will not flow. This is in part because Reiki has its own wisdom and again, is not our own energy that is given in a treatment. For this reason a Reiki practitioner will never be drained of energy after a treatment, they may be tired but only because they are relaxed like the client. Interestingly enough, in giving a Reiki treatment the practitioner also benefits and receives a certain healing component from Reiki simply by being part of the process of treating the client.

Reiki 'works' by sending energy to the places in the body that has energy blocks, since the Ki that is in us all flows through the body through pathways called chakras or meridians. At times these pathways can become blocked, and often as a result we feel pain or stiffness or tension in the area. Reiki heals by sending energy to open up those blocks and helping to rebalance the flow of our energy. "By flowing through the affected parts of the energy field and charging them with positive energy, Reiki raises the vibratory level in and around the physical body where the negative thoughts and feelings are attached. This causes the negative energy to break apart and fall away. In so doing, Reiki clears, strengthens and heals the energy pathways, thus allowing healthy Ki to flow in a natural way."[56] It has been used and documented in the cures of everything from headaches to broken bones and even cancer.

But what about the Placebo effect with Reiki? Like the Bach Flower Essences, that is the most common criticism of Reiki as well–that it doesn't really 'do' anything; 'it is all in the heads of the people', 'they weren't really sick to begin with', etcetera. There has however, been a significant amount of research done on Reiki practice, much to its favor. In fact, Reiki is currently used in over 100 hospitals in the USA (including the Manhattan Eye, Ear & Throat Hospital, Tucson Medical Centre in Arizona, California Pacific Medical Centre, and many others all over the map) and more Reiki clinics are beginning to open in Canadian hospitals as well.

> Independent research by Dr. Robert Becker and Dr. John Zimmerman during the 1980's investigated what happens whilst people practice therapies like Reiki. They found that not only do the brain wave patterns of practitioner and receiver become synchronized in the alpha state, characteristic of deep relaxation and meditation, but they pulse in unison with the earth's magnetic field, known as the Schuman Resonance. During these moments, the biomagnetic field of the practitioners' hands is at least 1000 times greater than normal, and not as a result of internal body current. Toni Bunnell (1997) suggests that the linking of energy fields between practitioner and earth allows the practitioner to draw on the 'infinite energy source' or 'universal energy field' via Shuman Resonance. Pro. Paul Davies and Dr. John Gribben in The Matter Myth (1991), discuss the quantum physics view of a 'living universe' in which everything is connected in a 'living web of interdependence'. All of this supports the subjective experience of 'oneness' and 'expanded consciousness' related by those who regularly receive or self-treat with Reiki.

> Zimmerman (1990) in the USA and Seto (1992) in Japan further investigated the large pulsating biomagnetic field that is emitted from the hands of energy practitioners whilst they work. They discovered that the pulses are in the same frequencies as brain waves, and sweep up and down from 0.3-30 Hz, focusing mostly in 7-8 Hz, alpha state. Independent medical research has shown that this range of frequencies will stimulate healing in the body, with specific fre-

---

56.   Ibid., 11.

quencies being suitable for different tissues. For example, 2 Hz encourages nerve regeneration, 7 Hz bone growth, 10 Hz ligament mending, and 15 Hz capillary formation. Physiotherapy equipment based on these principles has been designed to aid soft tissue regeneration, and ultra sound technology is commonly used to clear clogged arteries and disintegrate kidney stones. Also, it has been known for many years that placing an electric coil around a fracture that refuses to mend will stimulate bone growth and repair.

Becker explains that 'brain waves' are not confined to the brain but travel throughout the body via the perineural system, the sheaths of connective tissue surrounding all nerves. During treatment, these waves begin as relatively weak pulses in the thalamus of the practitioner's brain, and gather cumulative strength as they flow to the peripheral nerves of the body including the hands. The same effect is mirrored in the person receiving treatment, and Becker suggests that it is this system more than any other, that regulates injury repair and system rebalance. This highlights one of the special features of Reiki (and similar therapies)—that both practitioner and client receive the benefits of a treatment, which makes it very efficient.

It is interesting to note that Dr. Becker carried out his study on world-wide array of cross-cultural subjects, and no matter what their belief systems or customs, or how opposed to each other their customs were, all tested the same. Part of Reiki's growing popularity is that it does not impose a set of beliefs, and can therefore be used by people of any background and faith, or none at all.[57]

There are seven Chakras, the Root which is associated with the colour red and survival; the Sacral which is associated with the colour orange and sexual creativity; the Navel which is associated with yellow and identity; the Heart associated with green and pink, and naturally, love; the Throat associated with blue and expression; the 3rd Eye associated with indigo and the intuitive self; and the Crown associated with deep violet and white, and the divine. Also, Reiki is not just a hands-on practice. This is just the beginning, and in fact for most of a treatment practitioners will hold their hands a few inches away from or above the client's body in order to treat the aura as well. But with the second and third degrees of Reiki, practitioners can begin to do some really incredible things, like send energy to a person in a different location, as far away as the other side of the world, or to the past or the future, to help heal previous events or help out in

57. Tamisha Sabrina, UK Reiki Federation, "The Science Behind Reiki: What Happens in a Treatment?" *Canadian Reiki Association Newsletter*, January 2005, 5.

events to come. This type of Reiki is aided with the use of traditional symbols which are kept secret, out of respect for the practice.

It is important to explore the history of Reiki, especially its history in the West. Mrs. Hawayo Takata is responsible for bringing Reiki from Japan to the West in 1938. She was the only link in this part of the world until just recently, when some students visited Japan and discovered some discrepancies in her teachings. She was a Hawaiian woman who had a very difficult life and after suffering several years with ill health traveled to Japan in 1930 where her parents were originally from and had returned to. She learned of Reiki and went for regular treatments until, in a matter of months she was healed. So impressed with the results, Mrs. Takata studied Reiki herself and eventually was assisted by her Japanese Master/Sensei to establish a clinic in Hawaii and later elsewhere in the USA.

Mrs. Takata initiated students to level II Reiki all over the country as she traveled to heal and teach and she became a very well known healer. It was not until 1970 that she began initiating students to the Master level, and charged $10,000 for the two day attunement session. This expensive fee was never part of the Usui tradition, nor were her other teachings that a student, once initiated in Reiki must never go to another teacher. In addition, she taught her students to never give a treatment without being compensated for it and did not permit her students to take notes on anything she taught, including the symbols they were given beyond the first level. No one knows why Mrs. Takata chose to make these changes to the original Usui system from Japan, but recent studies and travels by Reiki practitioners have brought the more traditional methods and teachings of Japan to the West now, and so we know Dr. Mikao Usui's story.

Usui was born in 1865 in Japan, and is believed to have studied at a Tendai Buddhist school from a very young age. He also studied qigong, another healing practice that uses life energy. It was during a Isyu Guo, twenty one day course sponsored by the Tendai Buddhist Temple near Mt. Kurama in 1914 that he 'discovered' Reiki, or rather it is believed the Reiki energy entered his crown chakra. Naturally, there are parallels between the symbols and philosophy of Usui Sensei's system of Reiki healing and those of Kurama-Koyo Buddhists, formerly Tendai Buddhists.[58]

When he realized what Reiki could do, he began helping people, particularly the poor and also started teaching, or initiating others to begin practicing Reiki as well.

---

58.   Rand, *Reiki*, 24.

... in 1922, he moved to Tokyo and started a healing society which he named 'The Usui System of Reiki Healing.' ... The lowest degree of his training was called Shoden (First Degree) and was divided into four levels: Roku-To, Go-To, Yon-To, and San-To. (Note that when Mrs. Takata taught this level, she combined all four levels into one. This is why she did four attunements for level one.) The next degree was called Okuden (Inner Teaching) and had two levels: Okuden-Zenki (first part), and Okuden-Koki (second part). The next degree was called Shinpiden (Mystery Teaching) which is what we call master level.[59]

The symbols that Usui Sensei used were preserved and passed on to us in the West by Mrs. Takata–those she did keep the same, as was confirmed by Fumio Ogawa, a member of the Usui Reiki Ryoho Gakkai. When Usui Sensei died in 1926 of a stroke, a huge memorial was erected beside his grave by his students. "Mr. J. Ushida took over as president of the Usui Reiki Ryoho Gakkai."[60]

Animal Consciousness

So, now that we have explored these two 'alternative' forms of healing, vibrational medicine, we can contemplate what they have to contribute to the debate on animal consciousness. First of all, let us recap the kind of healing these medicines provide. Bach Flower Essences heal imbalances between the personality and the soul, thereby promoting increased physical health as a result. Reiki promotes relaxation and stress reduction and is by definition 'universal energy' that treats the highest good of a particular being. At the core of its philosophy is the existence and presence of a vital life force (which can be synonymous with the concept of 'soul', or spirit) existing in everything that is alive.

Already Reiki's philosophy identifies and promotes a certain level of equality in all living things which includes more than just humans and non-human animals, but fish, plants and birds too. If Bach Flowers 'work' with animals the same way they do with humans, then they too can be shown to promote an equality between 'them' and 'us' in that it requires the animals to have both a soul and a personality, as well as a 'higher good'.

So, do Reiki and Bach Flowers work for non-human animals like they do for humans? Absolutely. In fact, many would argue that both work BETTER for animals than people because their responses to these treatments are completely honest and unprejudiced. They cannot be told what is being given to them, it cannot

---

59. Rand, *Reiki*, 24.
60. Rand, *Reiki*, 25.

be explained to them like we explain it to each other and so we must accept their reactions as completely genuine to the effects of the healing of vibrational energy therapies. What's more, if it works for them, then there is significant evidence it is more than a 'placebo' and also, we can look at it to be evidence of yet greater spiritual, emotional and consciousness equality between 'them' and 'us' as these are the very elements that these vibrational therapies treat/heal.

The Evidence

While there are plenty of documented cases of both Bach Flower Essences and Reiki having profound effects on animals, I wanted to begin this testimonial evidence with a first hand experience. This is a story about a horse, to whom I am his 'person'. The horse, KC, has had an incredibly rough start to life. He belonged to a summer camp that gave their horses to volunteer keepers over the winter months in the off-season and in his very first winter, from the day he left his mother KC went to keepers who were not terrible people, but very inexperienced ones. They had never dealt with a baby horse before and so early on in their time looking after him were surprised to learn that he could kick. This is a typical occurrence for young horses since, just like small children, they need to be taught what is acceptable behavior at least in the presence of adults, and what is not. This is the simple adolescent phase KC was going through, but to his keepers it was very scary since he was a horse, and though still small was quite powerful. So, they locked him in a stall for the remainder of the winter months they had agreed to keep him for, instead of calling the camp and asking to be relieved of the responsibility.

This neglect is what they admitted to, but it does not account for the fact that when the camp horse staff went to get him in the Spring to travel back to the camp facilities he was so terrified of people in his stall that he literally fell to the ground when they touched him gently. Further, two very large indentations were on his rump, which a vet diagnosed as muscle tissue missing and suggested could have come from a very aggressive bite from another horse. This account for the missing muscle chunks in KC's hide is impossible though, as he had been kept in a stall all winter, with no exposure to other horses. We can only imagine how he received such significant injuries–the indentations have never healed, the muscle never returned even though he is now six years old.

So, the very beginning was terrifying for KC, and he was taught from a very early age to fear people. Later, multiple malignant cancer tumors were identified all over his body. At this point, he was three years old, and I officially 'owned' him, though I prefer to think of this transaction in terms of me simply becoming 'his person'. Either way, we were legally a team and his health was my responsibility. So, we went to the vet collage on Prince Edward Island for surgery to remove the tumors and charged it to my student loan. After a few weeks of being very sick after the surgery, he came around and had avoided ill health for some time.

However, this past Fall, just as I was beginning to seriously study both Reiki and Bach Flower Essences, KC came in from the pasture one day with a slight limp and a small cut on his left shoulder. We cleaned it and thought everything would be fine, but within four days it had swelled up to about the size of small pizza, and KC could hardly walk; in fact, he struggled even to hop on his three good legs and dragged the bad one. It was heart wrenching to watch. After cupfulls of puss and fluid oozed out of the tiny cut a few small bone chips were also flushed out. With several vet calls, an ultrasound and, series of x-rays the vets determined the mystery wound somehow penetrated the skin and muscle into the bone such that the infection itself had gotten into his humorous bone. I have provided this illustration of KC's background in order to establish a real sense of his emotional issues such that the subsequent results of his experience with vibrational medicine can be contextualized.

During this shoulder injury KC had to travel to the provincial vet office in order to have definitive x-rays and tests done. He is nervous of all people, but especially nervous of vets as he is terrified of needles and associates their typical attire with the painful pokes. So, prior to the trip I mixed him up a remedy of Bach Flower Essences. In it I included Mimulus for his know fears, Walnut for the change of location he would have to deal with, and Rescue Remedy for the stress of the experience altogether. I gave him 4 drops of this mix on sugar cubes 5 times throughout the day–before we left our barn, when we arrived at the clinic, when we left the clinic, when we got home and again later that night. It was absolutely amazing to watch him at the vet clinic. When in the previous vet visit we had, months prior just for his annual vaccines and booster shots he was rearing to get away from the needles and we had to tranquilize him just to give the shots. Also, before we went to the provincial vet we had his regular vet bring the portable ultrasound machine out to the barn to see if it would give us any further insight to what was going on inside his shoulder. He was terrified of it, and despite the fact he couldn't walk (taking 45 minutes to move about 20 feet), and was dragging his leg at the time he tried to run away from the ultrasound. Yet, with the Bach Flower Essences even in a whole new environment, with vets and overhead x-ray machines and lots of strange people he was like a totally different horse. He stood perfectly still, relaxed and confident in the examination room at the clinic and for the x-rays, and even for his needles. Even my friend who came for *my* emotional support couldn't believe what she witnessed in KC, he just wasn't expressing any of his usual fear in even the most potentially threatening environment he's been in, in a long time.

But the next part is even more incredible. After the final vet trip KC was prescribed heavy doses of antibiotics and estimated a minimum 4 months recovery period. So, we mixed his daily dose of 86 antibiotic pills with apple sauce to mask the horrible taste. But we also gave him weekly Reiki treatments and kept his name in a Reiki energy grid—a plate with stones charged regularly to send energy to the names and issues written down and placed in it, something like a continuous prayer or positive intention being sent out. There was definitely a lot of energy moving through his body during the Reiki treatments, and I frequently felt a static or buzzing feeling when I worked around his shoulder. He would always relax during treatments, and often nap afterwards. The most incredible result was that a full month before the vets thought KC would be able to start a walking exercise program, he was actually fully recovered—running, bucking and playing without a hint of lameness in the pasture. I don't doubt the antibiotics had a significant role to play in his recovery, but it was very clear to me that the combination of Reiki treatments and Bach Flower Essences dramatically improved the situations and healing process.

What's really fascinating is when the animals seek out Reiki treatments themselves. Chino, a cat my brother rescued as a kitten developed a bladder problem about 5 years ago. It got so bad that it was actually blocking his whole bladder and he couldn't urinate. When we discovered that he was in acute pain and realized that something was wrong, we immediately took him to the Clinic and were informed by the vets that they had to operate immediately, or he would die very soon. Naturally, we chose the surgery option and after a few weeks he was as good as new. Interestingly though, when my mother completed her first Reiki attunement and first offered the energy to Chino he did a very peculiar thing. While he is by nature a very cuddly cat, demanding at least an hour of undivided attention and affection a day, he makes it very clear he never wants anyone touching his tummy, and frequently will push your hand away with his paws if that is how you are holding him. But when Mom offered Chino Reiki for the first time, he came right to her and laid down in a very strange position on his back, positioning her hand on his lower belly, just over his bladder. Then he stayed just like that for about half an hour soaking up the energy. Never having done anything like this before, we are confident that it was a response to the energy that made Chino request the healing energy to go to the area that needed it most, from past trauma.

One more amazing Reiki account I would like to include is of a wild stag that Elizabeth Fulton describes in <u>Animal Reiki.</u> Elizabeth, a Reiki practitioner, found in her driveway one day a young stag. She was used to having deer in her yard as it seemed to be a popular green space for them to graze around her neighborhood, and a place they came to learn they were safe. But this one particular male deer just stood and stared at Elizabeth and eventually lifted one of his hind legs to reveal a wound. So she offered him Reiki and he continued to stand still for a period, and then shifted to move his injured leg closer to her. As she continued a treatment he lowered his head and seemed to be deeply relaxed and semi-dozing. He stayed for an hour, until Elizabeth ended the treatment because she had things to do. The next day the stag returned for treatment, twice and then again every day for several weeks until the wound had healed and he no longer had a limp. Clearly he was consciously experiencing and recognizing some benefit to these abnormal and prolonged periods of time spent in very close proximity to a human, a natural predator for a deer and especially when he was in such a vulnerable, injured state. This account makes it quite clear that not only can animals benefit from Reiki treatments, but they know it too.

Conclusions

So what does all of this mean with respect to the animal experimentation and consciousness debates? Well, clearly both Bach Flowers and Reiki work for animals just like they work for people. Similarly, the prominent and leading figures for both of these therapies welcomes and emphasizes that they do indeed benefit animals as well. So based on the philosophies of Reiki and Bach Flowers, if these therapies show physical healing in animals, then *they* must have personalities, emotions, and souls and must therefore with this combination posses consciousness. What's more, according to the philosophies and theoretical components of vibrational medicine, if it works on non-human animals, then they must not only have consciousness, but they must have a spiritual component to their lives considering these therapies treat the mind and soul first and the body second. Since vibrational therapies work with higher consciousness to promote healing, when we have evidence that they are equally effective in animals as they are in humans, the animals must have a sense of spirituality. And in order to contemplate, appreciate or even understand spirituality, we must have the consciousness to experience and recognize it. Animals must have both, according to virational medicine theory.

What's more, vibrational medicine heals emotional issues, which can be classified as 'mental stuff'. So if we notice a difference in the animal in relation to these types of treatments, it is them responding on an emotional and mental level to the Bach flowers and a higher, spiritual consciousness level for Reiki. If 'they' can feel and be healed by spiritual, universal energy they must also be connecting and resonating in harmony with 'us' and the earth, which suggests that we are all indeed spiritual equals, and so nonhuman animals should be respected as such. The use and equivalent effectiveness of Bach Flower remedies and Reiki for both humans and nonhuman animals suggests that indeed we are essentially the same with respect to possessing both consciousness and souls. Our energies are affected and healed the same way with vibrational energy, which again assumes and targets emotional, mental and spiritual components directly which subsequently affects our physical health. If our energy, our consciousness and our souls are all the same, then it can only be considered absolutely immoral to continue to subject non-human animals to experimentation, especially since the primary argument in support of animal experimentation is that 'they' are different from 'us' because they do not have souls and they do not have consciousness. Vibrational medicine and especially Bach Flower Essences and Reiki completely disqualify this justification, and subsequently all moral arguments in support of animal experimentation that use the premise that we are 'different' cognitively or spiritually.

Feminist Critiques of Science Contributes to the Debate:

✦

'Critters Have Feelings Too'

Non-human animals are used in experiments and toxicology testing rather than humans because there are simply too few human volunteers, and it is considered unethical to perform such tests on humans because human life is valued more by those who create the laws and sponsorship around this research. Non-human animals are used because our global society's demand for synthetic chemicals plays a significant role in the global economy, and since human-testing is unethical, non-human animals are the next closest thing. While it is recognized they have huge differences in their biological make-up from humans, those in favour of animal testing believe their similarities outweigh their differences. There are a large variety of animals and types of tests used for toxicology, which are designed to measure the level of toxicity a synthetic chemical has on a living organism, and how exactly it effects the organs and tissues of the exposed test subject.

Generally the Randomized Experimental Design (RED) is employed in toxicology testing, where two samples are drawn from a population of whatever the species of choice happens to be, and are studied over a period of time. Now, these two samples are groups of individuals. One group is the control group, which means they will not be exposed to any synthetic chemical for the study, and are used as a monitor to compare with the opposite, experiment group over the course of the testing. The experiment group is exposed to whatever chemical (generally it is only one chemical they are exposed to at a time, so as to be able to more clearly distinguish what caused any abnormalities, sicknesses or fatalities) the study was created for, by one of many methods.

The chemical could be given to the 'experimentees' orally, by way of injection, application topically to the skin, or eyes, nose, etc, or by polluting the air within their cages with the chemical of choice. Chemical application is done either in one single dose, or in regular doses over a long period of time. Every other aspect of the experiment group's lives are controlled, and kept exactly the same as the control group–the amount of time they are exposed to light and darkness, the size of their cages, what their cages are cleaned with, etc. This is so that at the end of the experiment the researchers can determine what was caused by the chemical exposure and what was "natural" for that particular species, in that circumstance.

Often high doses of the chemicals are administered to the group in a short amount of time and the experiment group is timed for how long it takes for one half of the group to die. This is called the LD 50 test (Lethal Dose for 50%, LD tests for different %s are also employed). Eventually all of the participants in this test will be killed, because the surviving 50% will be autopsied to determine exactly how the chemical affected the living beings, and what course it took through the body. Smaller doses are administered in other groups until they come to an amount where no observable effect comes from the experiment. (This could be done in again, one dose, or regulated doses over an extended period of time, depending on the chemical and the test employed in the study).

This number is then extrapolated to what the researchers believe to be a corresponding amount, safe for humans. This is done through a mathematical equation where the researchers estimate an extrapolation number they believe to be valid and multiply it with the no observable effect dose from the test species, to arrive at a dose that *should* hold no observable effects in humans. There are different calculation systems and extrapolation factors used by different researchers and programs, which makes this method less than perfect, at the very least.

Non human animals used for toxicology testing include all kinds of species, from fish to cats and dogs, to rabbits, to primates like monkeys and lemurs, but the most commonly used are rodents like rats and mice and guinea pigs. Rodents are most common for a number of reasons, partially because it is easier to present what most people consider to be "pests" to be socially acceptable for animal testing than it is for pets. This isn't the only reason, and thousands of pet species are still used annually, but rodents are also much easier and cheaper to care for in the research labs. They eat less, and require smaller spaces for living, plus they are cheaper to buy and faster reproducing, and therefore easier to track their genealogy. There are many "perks" but they do have a significantly shorter lifespan than humans, and are susceptible to different things than us. What's more, their bodies react to things differently than ours do, in a number of different ways, and so this certainly isn't the "perfect" candidate for toxicology testing. Still, in Canada, every year around 2 million animals are used in toxicology testing, and of that over 1.2 million are mice.

◆   ◆   ◆

There exists a fundamental dilemma in the debate over scientific experimentation on non-human animals which arises when two opposing arguments are offered to justify the same practice in different contexts. There is the argument for viability and value of such experimentation based on the fact that non-human animals are so much *like* humans physiologically, subsequently making great models for test subjects where we cannot use humans. This leads into the second argument: the idea we *can* use non-human animals for experimentation where it is unethical to use humans because they are so *different* from us that they should exist outside our moral sphere, so using them as test subjects is ethically "okay." This pair of arguments creates a never ending feedback loop–if they are so similar then how can it be ethical to use them? Because they are so different; but then, why use them as test subjects at all–will the experiments be able to tell us anything about ourselves? Yes, because their biological systems are so similar in kind to ours. Such statements could ping pong back and forth forever, the ultimate problem is that they contradict one another, yet are used to defend the very same thing.

This can perhaps be linked to the broader problem in science–its claim to be an objective search for the truth. When "proofs" are contradictory there is a problem, and when justifications for anything can be contradicted, values–unconscious or not–are illuminated. The fundamental dilemma of animal experimentation points to just one area in science that cannot claim to be value-free or value-neutral for there is enormous and intense opposition to this kind of work. This science cannot be value-free because it contradicts the values of all those who oppose it.

Feminist Critiques of science seek to open up the field of study to outside critique so that such controversial issues can be brought to light in an effort to improve the objectivity of science and get closer to the truth. As part of this goal feminists aim to achieve equality, thereby removing stereotypical, unconscious or not, race and gender biases from works and methods intended to be objective. In this sense, there are many parallels between where and how science has historically oppressed women, minorities, and non-human animals. For the purpose of this section we will look more closely at the links between women and animals in science and the fight for equality.

Lynda Birke said, "Tensions between similarity and difference are central to western feminist thinking."[1] So let's begin there, by further exploring the problems associated with similarities and differences that feminist critiques of science have observed. "... science tends to observe animals as exemplars in their sameness. They represent 'species horse'; but what is often missing from scientific accounts of the behavior of animals is an understanding of each one's uniqueness, of difference."[2]

When we suggest that an individual is always an accurate representation of a population or species we are generalizing to a point that is arguably dangerous in terms of investigative research. How often are two individual people exactly the same in terms of their physical appearance and their likes, dislikes, interests and opinions? How often are those of siblings, even identical twins? It is rare that we find humans as identical pairs let alone precisely representative of a whole population or our whole species. What is to say that non-human animals would be any different? When a dog has a litter of puppies even the ones that may look alike tend to have very different and unique personalities. The same is true of all other non-human animals that people have interacted with on an individual basis–animal "owners" or care takers are well aware of the uniqueness of different individual non-human animals–at least in the case of birds and mammals. Just ask any care taker at an animal hospital or pet store, or even the zoo–even if they do not have a particular fondness for the animals they work with, if they interact with them on a regular basis they will observe differences between individuals.

This is not to suggest that individuals cannot be representative of general characteristics of their species. Certainly we all exhibit a certain 'humanness', or 'horse-ness' for example, but just as no biology textbook's diagram of a human body is an exact illustration of every human body, no being should be viewed as an exact representation of their population or species. Diversity is the greatest protection from extinction every species has, even down to plant and bacteria life. To assume that any individual could be an exact replica of another is to assume it has artificial or inanimate qualities. However, embracing the differences individuals exhibit, allows for deeper and more intimate understanding of a whole species as any non-human animal trainer will tell you.

> As a scientist I have studied the behavior of animals as part of a group. This one is assumed to represent the species 'rat', that one, the species 'Bengalese finch'. Meanwhile, I was training horses; here it is not the representative animal I work with, but the individual, in all its glorious idiosyncrasy. And ... I

---

1. Linda Birke, *Feminism, Animals and Science: The Naming of the Shrew*, Open University Press 1994 Buckingham, 4.
2. Ibid., 4.

suspect I know more about the species horse–*Equus caballus*–than I do, in practice, about either finches or rats.[3]

So, we can see that there are certain limitations imposed on studies when assumptions are made that individuals are representative of species–in such practice of generalization we are only able to learn in a general sense, and are prevented from gaining knowledge on specifics or finer details. But how do generalizations come to exist in science? The language science employs is part of the problem. Through language, science has facilitated cultural intentions of separating ourselves from nature and constructing a linear hierarchy of species.

While attempting an objective view of the world, science (perhaps inadvertently) separates humans from nature. Science is a human construction, a field of study that is intended to help us find absolute truth about the world in which we live, about ourselves, and about things beyond even our own planet. But by being a human construction it has at its very heart, humans, who ultimately have values and beliefs. It is a difficult thing to separate ourselves from our own beliefs and be truly objective about anything, especially considering many of the values we hold are expressed subconsciously. So, in order to claim objectivity, scientists must attempt to remove their research from their personal views of the world, away from any biases and prejudices they may hold. This is proving to be easier said than done. There is a whole language set and writing style that scientists employ to try to eliminate 'themselves' from their work.

To explore exactly how science has been used to oppress, we must look at the language used in our culture and in science. By exploring the meanings behind language used by scientists we can reevaluate where objectivity is skewed–perhaps the problem is not in looking through the microscope, but rather in the linguistic description of the interpretations of what *is* observed where values leak into the picture. Certainly there are values held in the methods chosen for research as well, and these are points that also raise conflict; but looking at the language science uses or requires of its students we can gain insights to how science has been used to oppress women and animals at least in the Western world. Language has often been the focus of many arguments setting humans apart from all other species, (we are the only ones who can speak, that we know of) so I feel it is the perfect point for exploration to determine where and how we discriminate against other species as well as members of our own, in scientific studies.

---

3.   Ibid., 7-8.

To study science, or the 'nature' of something assumes a certain meaning behind the word 'nature'–first that this is the description of something constant and true, and second that 'nature' is 'natural', inevitably or innately so, without outside influence. As one can see, we are led to a philosophical place when we begin thinking about and constructing meanings of words. So, to study nature scientifically is to study the systems in nature–chemical elements, physical particles, or biological system functions like the nervous system or circulatory system. This practice is assumptive that all things are the sum of their parts, or of their biology. To study science then, is to study parts and assume knowledge of a collective whole based on the combination of the systems within it that 'make it work' as a whole.

This very practice holds a view that is designed to be value free, but must inherently carry values because it remains unattractive and controversial to many who feel the need to study the bigger picture to gain a complete understanding of a subject. This is one element of science that feminist critiques illuminate as problematic. Birke admits,

> ... how we see, or use ideas about, animals and their similarity or difference from us, and the relationship between that set of ideas and debates about feminism and science ... like other feminists who are also scientists, my own experience has been of unease: how can I think as a feminist while at the same time be a scientist? ... trying to be both sometimes felt impossible.[4]

Evelyn Fox Keller wrote, "As both a feminist and a scientist, I am more familiar than I might wish with the nervousness and defensiveness that such a potential conflict evokes."

> Yet that has not been the only source of potential conflict for me. The choice to study biology was never straightforward. On one hand, I liked science and was passionate about natural history, but on the other, I recognized that doing biology would mean doing experiments with animals. I did do biology, and so had to try to live with the moral conflicts ever since. I have always had qualms about the moral 'rightness' of whatever it was I was doing, and I continue to have doubts about the ways in which science uses animals. Those may be doubts shared with many scientific colleagues for many reasons, but for me they are partly feminist doubts.

---

4.   Ibid., 6.

I found it peculiar that the love of nature that, in part, drove me to want to study biology seemed at odds with the scientific methods in which I was trained. Loving nature meant a respect for its complexity, yet to do science means to accept its reductionism.... the living animal becomes coded as an assemblage of its parts, as machine-like: 'Living Control Systems', 'Nerve, Muscle and Synapse' ... Doing science often meant awe at the wonderful ways that such 'systems' worked; nature was, indeed, very clever. But it also seemed to mean denying the awe at the marvelous creatures that exist in the world, in all their complexity and individuality.[5]

Science reduces nature to the sum of its parts, living things to a collection of interconnected systems that combine to facilitate life, by engaging in the process of naming and categorizing through taxonomy. So, written descriptions of components of individual species are identified, documented and given a title. Individual species are given names, a scientific one, and a common one typically. Then, different species who share enough of the same systems or physiological components are grouped together in another classification level. The top level is a 'Kingdom' which has subsets of 'Phyla'; each 'Phyla' consists of 'Classes' which contain 'Families' that can, in turn, be broken down to the 'Genus' and finally, the smallest grouping is the 'Species'. Note the resemblance of a hierarchical trend in this classification process. Note also, this system does not recognize individuals within a species–there is no category for them.

There is still a generalizing limitation in this classification process though. "Scientific naming of animals gives them a species and describes them as such, who or what they are as individuals matters little for these purposes."[6] This whole practice is one that feminists principles tend to conflict with, and is an area in science where parallels between women and non-human animals can be found. "... science has sought to name both animals and women. Naming, feminists have stressed, is a powerful process. In scientific accounts, women too have been described as being limited by their biology."[7] So, in essence then, the feminist fight against suggestions from science like this, must also oppose such suggestions of non-human animals.

"A central plank of feminist criticism of the sciences has been that science has, generally, had rather little respect for people. We have focused ... on derogatory statements made by biologists about women's nature ... But science also has little respect for the non-humans it studies."[8] Perhaps this lack of respect is the out-

---

5. Ibid., 7.
6. Ibid.
7. Ibid.

come of attempted objectivity, but it can more accurately be attributed to andro-centric cultural biases. When the vast majority of people trying to be objective are 'generally' the same (namely affluent white men), it seems since they share the same value system it is difficult for any to identify unconscious prejudice or bias seepage into their scientific interpretations of observations and the subsequent results. In trying to objectify their interpretations of research animals, scientists have actually only succeeded in treating the individuals *as* objects. "In the labora-tory, … animals tend to become numbers and codes; rat 23/5A/F is just another rat in the experimental design."[9]

Take for example a particle experimentation in which animal test subjects continued to die, not because of the experiments done to them, but because they were placed in an air-tight cage for the experiment–researchers were so caught up in objectivity they forgot the animals they were experimenting with were actually living, breathing animals, and had treated them as inanimate objects of study. Here, animals were objects, possessions, things 'designed' for humans to use. This philosophy has also been used to justify human slavery, and suppress women under their fathers and husbands as something less than human by religious or cultural standards. These are recent practices in our Western world too, less than 100 years ago they all existed. Women were not permitted the right to vote in Canada until 1916, through the efforts of Nellie McClung, and even then it was not all women who got to vote. Women did not become 'persons' by law in Can-ada until England's Privy Council declared it so in 1929 because of the efforts of Emily Murphy, Nelly McClung, Henrietta Muir Edwards, Louise McKinney and Irene Parlby. Even human slavery existed legally in North America until the 1800's. When it is morally unjust, or unethical in any one of these cases, why should it not be so for the others?

A significant place in science that tends to perpetuate the human and andro-centric superiority complex, where we find parallels with oppression of women and nonhuman animals, exists in biological determinism. Feminist critiques of this science condemn "naïve biological accounts of women's (or anybody else's) behavior and capabilities. Biological accounts typically see gender as fixed–and fixed within cultural stereotypes. Feminists … object to both the stereotypes and the portrayal of them as biologically inherent."[10] Again we have an argument that has come to be accepted by the general public of our culture–though it has only

---

8.   Ibid., 8.
9.   Ibid., 8.
10. Ibid., 11.

been so for a few decades, women are viewed as equals now to men. There was a time when this wasn't so, just as there was a time in our society that racism and slavery was legally condoned. This is evidence of culture influencing scientific studies, when society largely accepted male supremacy scientific findings reflected these views, offering that women were in fact biologically determined to be something less than their male counterpart. This cannot be considered an objective search for the truth with such value laden undercurrents.

It has been progressive and positive, most would argue, that we have worked to remove these prejudices from our culture. Why should we not do the same for nonhuman animals?

> ... the notion that animals are little more than their biology; this is what constitutes their animalness. But if so, then we are inevitably going to face problems; analogies *are* drawn between human society and that of other species ... So, if animals are 'mere' biology, puppets of their genes, then there will inevitably be inferences made about the mere biology at the heart of human nature.[11]

Ultimately, we need to arrive at an understanding that, "to accept some similarity to other species is not necessarily to reduce or demean women (or humans more generally). Nor should we see nature as inherently fixed, while we take on ourselves the mantles of free will and social construction. Both, I believe, are misleading."[12]

> One reason why feminists have not been quick to debate the ethics of animal use in science has to do with our unease about talking about animal issues at all, for it has too often been the case that those people lacking power have been derogated by likening them to 'animals'. To be likened to 'an animal' in our culture is to be diminished, or to be mindlessly out of control, and who wants to be like that?[13]

This is an incredibly profound issue for two reasons. First, we have come to use animal 'names' as insults against other people, especially women.

> Images of animals ... are also invoked to describe women: I may thus become a chick, a bunny, a pussy (or, when I'm answering back, a bitch–or shrewish).

---

11. Ibid., 11.
12. Ibid., 13.
13. Ibid., 10.

> These words, of course, are intended to denigrate women, to reduce us 'to the level of beasts'. What is invoked is invariably a hierarchy: men above women, women above animals/nature.[14]

There is a science/culture feedback loop of disrespect and hierarchy. To suggest a man is feminine is to insult him with reduction to a lower status, similarly to suggest a woman is like an animal is to reduce her to an even lower status as well. Thus our daily speech perpetuates and condones the separation of humans from nature and men from women which science uses to justify its experimentations while simultaneously reinforcing the social consequences of such values. When these values are held publicly, it becomes difficult for anyone to 'see' their presence in scientific 'discoveries' or observations as it is difficult to recognize our own values unless they are in conflict with different ones. It is important then, in the true search for an objective truth, to open up all scientific research methods and results to critique from outside sources. The more diverse a group observing science, the more unconscious values will be illuminated simply by conflicting with those of a critic. In order for science to be truly objective and value neutral, it must not conflict with any values, not just appease the values of one particular group or culture. This is precisely what Feminist Critiques of Science has been arguing.

Second, it seems rather bizarre that in one context we as a whole culture come to hold such terminology as derogative slander against each other only to turn around and accept evolutionary accounts of scientific study that propose animal societies in 'nature' as explanations or justifications for much of the behavior that exists in human society. Such logic is known as the Naturalistic Fallacy. The idea has been used frequently in history, but is particularly noticeable in Darwin's works as much of his research suggested evidence in nature of androcentrism that both reflected and supported society at his time–Victorian England. Ruth Hubbard, a significant contributor to the Feminist Critiques field, points to several examples where Darwin's theory of evolution illustrates the ways in which sexist attitudes have shaped research conclusions by scientists. She notes that, "Science is made by people who live at a specific time in a specific place and whose thought patterns reflect the truths that are accepted by the wider society."[15] She

---

14.   Ibid., 17.
15.   Ruth Hubbard, "Have only Men Evolved?" In *Biological Woman—The Convenient Myth: A Collection of Feminist Essays and a Comprehensive Bibliography*, edited by Hubbard, Ruth.; Henifin, Mary Sue.; and Fried, Barbara. Cambridge, MA: Schenkman Pub. Co., 1982, 153.

points out that Darwinism, which is often thought of as being unique in history, has wide areas of congruence with social and political ideologies of 19th C Britain with Victorian precepts of morality, particularly between the sexes. She says that the same Victorian notions still dominate contemporary biological thinking about sex differences and sex roles.

An interesting study done with meercats illustrates this point. Researchers observed groups of meercats in their natural environments and determined that these animals show altruism in groups as a result of their observations of the meercat behavior. This conclusion was reached because different individuals would 'take turns' according to the research, breaking from digging for food to stand guard against predators. If an individual on guard saw a predator it would sound a warning call to the rest of the group and head for the burrow for safety. Such studies are then used to 'explain' why there is altruism in human family or friend groups–it fits under the premise 'it's only natural, because it happens in nature'. First of all, such premise is considered the 'naturalistic fallacy' and is hardly justifiable evidence for any behavior. What is even more interesting is the fact that when this study was repeated, researchers found opposite results. The very same behavior in the meercats was observed but this time scientists considered the 'on guard' behavior to be 'selfish' because none of the individuals who were on guard while a predator came into the scene was killed, in fact they were the first ones into the burrow. If science is truly objective, how could the same study have lead researchers to 'see' two different things? And why did the meercat behavior have to be considered selfish or altruistic at all? The evidence suggests simply that the individuals went on guard when they were full and went off guard when they were hungry again. This would have been a more objective conclusion to both of the studies done.

> How we view animal societies inevitably reflects the ways in which we experience our own: ... study of primate societies has incorporated the social and political assumptions of gender, race and class that inform the wider culture, and scientific accounts of other species which build upon cultural beliefs about gender and sexual orientation. Scientific accounts in turn feed back into the wider cultural consciousness ... they also incorporate and reinforce prevailing beliefs about masculinity and femininity.[16]

Other examples illustrative of scientific anthropomorphism occur in P.J.B. Slater's *Essentials of Animal Behavior*. One case shows three different types of

---

16. Birke, *Feminism, Animals and Science*, 10-11.

actions by cats that may appear 'aggressive' but it also suggests that the causes are likely different and therefore limiting their meanings to only aggression would be an oversight. It does, however, suggest that in each act–defending itself from a corner position, pouncing on a mouse, or 'territorial disputes'–the attempt of the cat is to "inflict harm on other individuals".[17] Why would such an assumption be reached when at least one alternative is available? Perhaps the cat in each of these situations is simply trying to survive; if it could do so without inflicting harm on another individual it may well take that option, but it has to eat, and it has to avoid predation, and it has to have a place to live in order to survive. Why is the intent determined to be one of cruelty when it could instead be one of necessary self-service, and strictly survival strategy.

Another case Slater's book describes is the famous study done by Harry Harlow with rhesus monkeys to determine why babies develop attachment to their mothers. Baby rhesus monkeys were taken from their mothers at very early ages and put in cages with two 'fake' mothers. One was a wire structure containing a milk bottle, the other was a softer, 'cuddly cloth-covered model mother'. This experiment was designed to determine whether babies seek their mothers out of biological necessity, for food and sustenance, or if it is more of an emotional cause behind infant attachment to their mothers. To test the theory, the baby monkeys had equal access to both substitute mothers and were intentionally scared to measure which 'mother' they sought for comfort. The babies clung to the soft cuddly mother in these situations, and "if the two [mothers] were close together they learned to cling to the cuddly one and lean across to drink from the other. Rhesus monkeys therefore become attached to their mothers without the need to be fed by them, and they use them as bases from which to explore."[18]

The Feminist arguments have pull with the evidence of this experiment in that it illustrates animals are indeed more than the sum of their biology–the baby monkeys sought comfort from a structure that provided no biological security of food or nutrients. One may argue that there was biological motivation for this choice in that the comfort of the soft monkey may have stimulated releases of certain chemicals in the brain that made the babies feel good–dopamine for example. However, such stimulation could just as easily have been triggered by the wire mother-substitute through similar contact with the baby if it were in fact, mere contact that caused such stimulation of brain chemistry. But the baby monkeys sought something soft and warm, which offered no more protection or sur-

---

17. P.J.B. Slater, *Essentials of Animal Behavior*, University Press, Cambridge: 1999, 63.
18. Slater, *Essentials of Animal Behavior*, 105.

vival value than the other, wire option. Why? Because there is more substance to the baby monkeys than a simple drive to nourish their biological symptoms. The conclusion is that the warmth and security that mothers supply their infants is what forms the basis of attachment, not food.

Slater's work also describes how male lions 'slaughter the dependent young fathered by' the previous male of the pride immediately after acquiring dominant male status within the group. He suggests that this is done for biological advantage,

> ... it benefits the males themselves. They may only be able to control the pride for a short time and the more young they have during that period the more of their genes they will be passing on. By killing cubs that they did not father, they make the mothers stop lactating and become receptive and thus speed on the time when these females will bear cubs sired by themselves ... for if cubs are not well grown by the time their fathers in turn get ejected, they too will be slaughtered and the whole investment wasted. In this way infanticide ... can be understood as of advantage to the individual, though it would certainly not be to the group or the species.[19]

This assumes biological determinism; that the cognitive and biological goal of every male lion is to pass on its own genes to as many offspring as possible. But this is a very poor evolution strategy of the species as a whole, as is suggested in the excerpt itself. Since biological diversity is the greatest defense any species can have, the practice of infanticide by male lions limits this possibility. It also assumes that the male lions either have absolutely no cognitive abilities outside instinctive impulses to achieve a sense of vicarious immortality through creation of multiple offspring, or that they consciously think about or strategize how they can ensure the presence of their personal genes in the most possible babies. Both of these options seem weak, and improbable in my opinion.

In his article, "How Do Animals Do Business?", Frans B. M. de Waal outlines a number of examples that point to evidence 'in nature' of how human economic behavior, particularly the underlying reasons behind our tendencies to exchange both resources and services, has evolved the way it has. It suggests that our economic behavior may not be entirely human, but rather a primate evolution strategy. There is a new theory of "Behavior Economics" which suggests human economic tendencies are not species specific and have evolved in other group dwelling primates as well; this theory says that economics are not based on greed,

---

19. Slater, *Essentials of Animal Behavior*, 151.

but as a result of the desire to "fit in" with the group and work toward collective survival. Animal behavioral economics suggests that reciprocity, division of rewards, and cooperation are not limited to human economic tendencies. It is likely these practices evolved in other species as well because of the opportunity they provide to maximize individual gains from social relationships without becoming detrimental to the group.[20]

The theory predicts that we can look at different non-human primate species and find similar economic tendencies between them and us. A number of experiments were carried out in order to test this prediction, each with a slight variation, or more specific articulation of this general prediction. In one experiment with capuchin monkeys who had been "taught to reach a cup of food on a tray by pulling on a bar attached to the tray" the theory was tested in the areas of cooperation and reciprocity. Several variations of this kind of test were recorded. One specific case paired two females in adjoining cages. By making the tray, on which the food rewards are placed, too heavy for one monkey to move alone, the monkeys quickly discovered they would have more success if they worked together. In one case, one of the monkeys–A (in sticking with scientific trend we will 'name' the monkeys arbitrarily with letters, as they did in this study)–in the test pair took the cup of food on her side of the tray and let go of the bar, releasing the tray, before her partner (B) had taken the other food cup. While monkey A ate the food she collected after completing the task of pulling the tray monkey B demonstrated quite clearly and loudly that she was not happy with not having been able to collect the reward that had been on her side of the tray. When monkey A finished eating the food she had taken from the tray she proceeded to work with monkey B to pull the tray again so monkey B could obtain her share of the food. Researchers conducting this test concluded that monkey A's behavior seemed to be a reaction to monkey B's objection to the loss of expected reward.[21] They suggest that this type of action is very similar to human economic transactions and is evidence of "cooperation, communication and the fulfillment of an expectation, perhaps even a sense of obligation."[22]

Behavior Economics theory offers evidence the economic tendencies of reciprocity and gratitude between the chimpanzees are very much the same as they occur in our own species. "This reciprocity mechanism requires memory of previous events as well as the coloring of memory such that it induces friendly behav-

---

20.   Frans B.M. de Waal, "How Animals Do Business" *Scientific American* April 2005 Vol. 292, No.4: 74.
21.   Ibid., 74.
22.   Ibid., 74.

ior. In our own species, this coloring process is known as 'gratitude,' and there is no reason to call it something else in chimpanzees."[23]

Partner choice is very important to behavioral economics because of its necessity to reciprocity.[24] Nonhuman primates, namely chimpanzees, have been observed to interact in a sort of "marketplace of services" as it is referred to in *Chimpanzee Politics* by Frans B. M. De Waal that rests on the interactions of individuals exchanging different sorts of 'currencies' between different partners "such as grooming, sex, support in fights, food, babysitting and so on."[25] With this sort of market place, individuals have the option of selecting partners as well as offering their own services for some variety of payment. This sort of structure for understanding reciprocity becomes economical and relates to supply and demand, which is what Ronald Noe and Peter Hammerstein of the Max Planck Institute for Behavioral Physiology in Seewiesen, Germany based their Biological Market Theory on.[26]

The Biological Market theory becomes applicable when partners of trade have the opportunity to choose the individuals they may work with and predicts that the value of both commodities and partners is determined by the availability of these resources.[27] One study for the Biological market theory looked at babies in baboon populations. In the case of baboons, most females are very much like human women in that they are very interested in babies, their own and even those of strangers. Baboon mothers are very protective of their newborns, and do not commonly make them available to other individuals. Female baboons have been observed to groom other females with babies, 'sneaking' views of the baby around its mother in the process. These grooming sessions often result in the mother becoming more willing to let her groomer observe her baby. The outside female is said to 'buy time' with the baby. These observations led researchers to suggest that in one study of wild chacma baboons in South Africa, troops with rare infants gave mothers the ability to place a greater value and 'price,' such as extended grooming, on time other females could spend with her baby, than mothers in a troop with many babies could.[28]

Another study looked more closely at the element of cooperation in nonhuman primates. In order for cooperation to be a beneficial economic tool, the indi-

---

23. Ibid., 76.
24. Ibid., 76.
25. Ibid., 77.
26. Ibid., 77.
27. Ibid., 77.
28. Ibid., 77.

viduals involved would have to keep track of the amount of effort each co-worker contributes and compare the reward distribution to ensure "fair play". This study focused on capuchin monkeys again to determine if animals do such monitoring. The study was developed based on field observations of the natural labor market these monkeys interact in; hunting and sharing giant squirrels. The prediction is that if cooperation is a behavior economic strategy that capuchin monkeys utilize when an individual captures some form of food with the help of others but keeps it solely for themselves, you can expect that there will be less interest and effort by other individuals to help them in the future. This sub-theory holds that capuchins engage in sharing hunted food because of the same logic chimpanzees and humans do—without shared rewards there will not be combined efforts in the hunt.[29]

The experiment attempted to mimic the natural group hunting scene to observe the capuchin's tendencies. They used the tray-pulling strategy by caging two individuals simultaneously, making the tray too heavy for one individual to pull alone, and only making a food cup available to one of the pair ('the winner'). If the winner was able to get the food, it would have only been made possible if the other ('the laborer') worked for the benefit of the winner. Note that previous tests showed the food possessing monkeys sometimes brought their food to the partition between the cages and allow the other monkey to take some, and on very rare occasions the possessor physically offered pieces of food to the other. To make this study relevant, researchers looked for new results, recording and comparing collective versus solo pulls.[30] This was achieved by setting different work patterns. Either the tray was too heavy for a single individual and both capuchins had access to a pull bar, or the tray was light enough for one individual and only the winning monkey had access to a pull bar.

The results showed more accounts of food sharing after team labour tests than after solo labour tests. They concluded that compensation was being granted to partners by winners, for the assistance they provided.[31] It was determined that sharing of rewards does in fact affect future cooperation efforts. Researchers found that the success rate of a team would decrease when the winner neglected to share, and subsequently determined that such 'payment' of labour assistance was an intelligent strategy.[32]

---

29. Ibid., 78.
30. Ibid., 78.
31. Ibid., 78.
32. Ibid., 78.

Sarah F. Brosnan studied further the division of rewards and the reactions this evoked from individuals in a group or pair. She employed a sort of currency between herself and the monkeys where she would give a capuchin monkey a pebble and then display a piece of cucumber as a reward for them to return the pebble. The focus here is on the principle of exchange. In adjoining cages a pair of capuchin monkeys seemed content to exchange their pebble currency for cucumber with the researcher. The test comes when the researcher offers one monkey a much more desirable food, grapes for example, in exchange for their pebble, but not the other monkey. The Behavior Economic Theory predicts that since the human tendency is to reject unequal pay, and because this theory is that human economic tendencies are not species specific, you can expect to find rejection of unequal pay with the capuchin study of exchange principles.

The researcher observations of this study were of significant changes in the capuchin monkey's willingness to participate in the exchange when the monkey in the cage adjacent to them was offered the more preferable food and they were not. Common response was not simply exchange reluctance, but many individuals displayed their agitation by throwing their pebbles and sometimes their cucumber slices out of their cages. Rejecting unequal pay is something humans do as well, but it is not in alignment with the theory of traditional economics. However, behavioral economics theory factors in evolutionary development of emotions and their substantial influence on behavior. "Discouraging exploitation is critical for continued cooperation."[33]

As a general conclusion, behavior economics addresses the problem of having to exert a lot of effort constantly monitoring benefits and favors, and answers it with the "buddy system". It suggests that our desire to form a few strong relationships with close friends and spouses for example, is an evolutionary strategy for protection against freeloaders and exploitation. Developing a few relationships that prove trustworthy over time allows us to relax our economic monitors so that these relationships are "relatively immune to inequality".[34] In more distant partnerships, with strangers or mere acquaintances for example, we continue our mental records of favors and benefits which justify stronger reactions to "unfair" practices. The series of non-human primate studies described above and in this article provide reason to believe, according to researchers, that similar, if not identical, strategies are practiced in more than just the human species.

---

33. Ibid., 78-9.
34. Ibid., 79.

The general message of this larger theory and the many experiments and studies conducted within it may be nice for the animal equality debate–it says humans and animals are similar. However, the underlying theme of each of the experiments outlined here was a justification of human behavior based on what is observed to occur in 'nature'. Its' very goal is to find evidence of human economic systems in nature to justify them as 'only natural' and therefore good and ethical. The problem is that it falls victim to the naturalistic fallacy just like Darwin's famous works 'observed' androcentric structure in just about every 'wild' species he studied which then appeared reflective of his own Victorian society's male supremacy.

When we look to nature for evidence of our own behavior tendencies, biases or prejudices, the science conducted must be 'tainted' with values. To suggest that because something can be 'observed' in nature it must be 'natural' and therefore inherently just or ethical is equivalent to a child's defense of doing wrong because, "he did it first!" There are many other explanations for the nonhuman primate behaviors in the studies outlined above than evolutionary economic strategy. There is no need to impose human qualities on the animals such as kindness or aggressive, selfishness or altruism, winner or labourer. To view them as such is self-serving for humans.

If science were truly objective it would observe the behavior in these studies as exactly what it is without any additional inferences; the monkeys were responding to the wild or artificial conditions they were in, such that they would sometimes take all available food for themselves and other times they would help or work with other individuals to share the food rewards of their efforts. Objectivity is lost when we begin assuming beyond the facts. The same is true in the case of the mothers 'sharing' their babies with other females who seem interested in them. How did the researchers see grooming actions as payment or currency in exchange for time with the baby when it could just as easily have been understood as something different? Perhaps the other females offer grooming to mother chimpanzees to prove they are kind and gentle and not a threat to the newborns. This reasoning would support the observations of 'higher' value on infants when there are fewer of them too, instead of the infants having a 'market value' for their mothers, perhaps the mothers are simply more protective of the infants since there are fewer of them and subsequently danger increases when there are fewer babies for predators to choose from. It could be argued that if more predator attention goes to individual infants when there are fewer of them, the mothers must be more protective of their babies to ensure their safety and therefore require more proof of other females' gentleness and safety. Perhaps this is altogether false, the point is that there are other options of explanation for non-human primate behavior, so for scientists to arrive at any single conclusion, based on the studies outlined above, cannot be truly objective.

These studies do however, point to the similarities in humans and nonhuman animals which is important. It offers that they *could* be like us, right down to our economic strategies. If this is possible, then one has a platform on which to rest an argument for treatment of nonhuman animals as equals within our moral sphere. If it is possible that they have these similarities, though we cannot prove them, we should give them 'the benefit of the doubt' and offer them the same ethical protection against pain and suffering as we do ourselves. Women and other races have been in the past considered something 'less human' than white men, but we have progressed past those mindsets (at least in the Western world); we now recognize they were wrong in both a literal and a moral sense. The arguments for and against nonhuman animal equality are the same, the debate is intensely similar, so if we were wrong before in failing to permit equality, what is to say we are not wrong again now?

An important issue that must be outlined here is the human tendency or intention of trying to separate itself from nature in order to achieve scientific objectivity. While this may be a well intentioned pursuit it may also be impossible. How could it be that we can remove ourselves, from ourselves? The prevalent Western cultural worldview is one of human superiority, of dominance and exploitation of the world. We see everything as either having been placed here by a creator for our own use, or that we are the most intelligent beings and therefore have the right to use and exploit all that is here in the name of science, to better understand it. Either way, the common view is that nature belongs to us, to do with what we please. But this view is fundamentally flawed. It forgets, or omits the factor that humans are part of that nature. *It* is bigger than us, and we are merely components within it. "'Nature' in this context of dominance is partly non-human nature–the other species of animals, the plants, the microorganisms, the geological structures of the earth–but it is also significantly much of human-ity."[35] To assume we have superiority and dominion over our whole planet or universe is at the very least a delusion of grandeur!

Language has played a key role in how science has been "gendered"–how it has come to be believed that objectivity can be achieved by eliminating empathy, gentleness, emotion, warmth and what it means to be 'feminine' from science and accepting/training scientists that to be cold, hard, unsympathetic, 'tough'

---

35. Birke, *Feminism, Animals and Science*, 11.

and 'masculine' is to be objective. Why is this necessary? If we have reached the conclusion that we as humans are more than the sum of our systems and parts, we are more than our biology, why would we think that we should use only half of our available qualities to research our world, the very thing we are part of. To remove ourselves from the elements of study and to remove our emotions from ourselves is to remove something that is potentially *necessary* in order to uncover certain 'truths' about 'nature'.

Where did the idea that we need to stand on the outside and look *in,* without feeling in order to see the truth come from? Is it not true that only when we observe each other and open our hearts to other people that we reveal our whole selves and subsequently tend to provoke a part of the other person to expose itself to us that would otherwise have remained hidden behind a biological front? We know that more than biology affects our day to day life as people, that parts of 'nature' evoke feeling and emotion in us. Seeing a kitten play makes us laugh, smelling a flower makes us smile, being yelled at makes us sad or angry, being trapped in a storm makes us scared. The Psychology Principle of Reciprocation holds that we feel obligated or compelled to mimic the same behavior or attitudes as those others display when we interact with them. When we are confronted with cold, hard things we tend to reflect that in our reactions, it is only when we are exposed to soft, warm things that we tend to show the 'soft, warm' qualities of ourselves. Life is interactive. Emotions are part of life. *We* are part of nature. So how can we expect to unveil the absolute truth without incorporating those two fundamental elements–ourselves and our emotions? Just as we inevitably invoke in others an element of themselves by showing emotion, perhaps we can observe another element of various species and nature as a whole by incorporating emotion in our studies of it. Why does being objective necessarily mean void of emotion? There is an inherent difference between emotions and values or beliefs. Emotions are reactive and innate. Values may determine which reactions are invoked in us, but they are not innate, they are learned.

Eating Our Pets & the Carcinogenic Consequences

"Heart Attack: God's punishment for eating his little animal friends."

—Don Tolman

While the general public of North America, Europe, Australia and Asia may or may not be aware of, or for that matter care about, the ethical horrors that take place in slaughterhouses for various types of meat for human consumption, those who are consumers of the end product need to be made aware of the serious health risks they are exposed to simply by having dinner! It's true there are very strict rules and restrictions around the health of the animals intended for slaughter for human consumption but the inspections of the animals often tend to either overlook or simply ignore what chemicals these animals could be carrying in their flesh because the health standard seems to be based primarily on the animals' physical appearance. This may be sufficient for cows, pigs, chickens, and other animals that are raised for the sole purpose of slaughter for human consumption, but what about horses?

Most of the North American population is unaware of the fact that millions of domestic horses from racetracks, show rings, or owners' backyards end up in one of several slaughterhouses between Canada, the United States and Mexico alone, not to mention those horses on the other side of the globe destined for the two in Austrailia. This makes up a small part of the global economy, with a few companies making a lot of money in a far from elegant business.

> In 1996, according to the USDA, the United States exported 38 million pounds of horse, ass, and mule meat, with a value of $64 million. Of the total volume exported in 1996, 29 million pounds, or 76%, went to Belgium and France. (The American Horse Council estimates that there are 6.9 million horses in the United States.)[1]

---

1.   Les Sellnow. "Lined for Slaughter". *The Horse: Your Guide to Equine Health Care Magazine*, (December 1999): 25.

The fact of the matter is that horses are a rather expensive "pet" and often when they are no longer performing to the standards of their owners, or bringing in a big enough pay cheque, owners feel the need to dispose of them.

The "humane" method of euthanasia for these unwanted, but not useless, horses is often both an unwanted expense for the owner followed by an additional responsibility and possible further expense of disposing of the horses' bodies. For these reasons it is not a common choice, especially in the winter when it is even more difficult to dig a hole big enough in the ground for burial. There is another option of sending the horses for meat for pet food and glue, but the horse must not have been euthanized, for reasons of transferring the lethal dose of drug from the horses' bodies to the animals that would then be eating their flesh, however the horse must still be dead before these pet food companies will accept them. On top of that, it is the owners' expense to have their dead horse delivered to these factories.

A couple of options remain for horse owners who no longer want, or are able to keep their horses for whatever reason, and often these options end with the horse in the same place: the slaughterhouse. Owners may sell their unwanted horses directly to a "meat buyer" or, they have the option of trying to sell their horse either privately, which takes time and they continue to have the expense of the horse until they can find a new owner, or they can sell their horse in an auction. Hundreds of horse auctions take place every year, all over the world and owners have no say in who makes the winning bid on their unwanted horses. "Meat buyers" often travel from auction to auction buying these horses for cheap prices and then reselling them to slaughterhouses for a profit.

The trouble with this is that they often don't make it known what their purpose for buying is, nor do they contact the previous owners to learn what the current health conditions of the horses are, or what medications they may have been on recently. This is the major concern with domestic horses headed for slaughterhouses, since many commonly used equine veterinary drugs are clearly labeled "do not use on horses intended for slaughter" and have withdrawal periods for horses that will be used for meat. If the "meat buyer" remains uninformed of the drugs the horses he/she purchases have been exposed to, they are going to go on to sell these horses to slaughterhouses with the mutual understanding that the horse is chemical-free and safe for human consumption as long as they meet the physical health inspection standards before they receive a nail, or bullet to the head.

The problem is that when there are no laws or regulations requiring blood or tissue samples from each of these domestic horses to test for various medications in the horse flesh that is intended for human consumption, the human consumers are at a very real risk of exposure to known human carcinogens and other pesticides! Loving horse owners who may not want to, but are forced to sell their horses will more than likely administer, or have veterinarians administer regular medications to their horses for health purposes such as de-wormers or vaccinations, or perhaps the horse needed to be treated with an antibiotic, anti-inflammatory agent, or pain killer. If owners don't know that the highest bidder in the auction ring is a "meat buyer" they may end up on the dinner table in a European or Asian country full of chemical carcinogens for their consumer.

There are many owners, loving or not, who end up desperate to sell their horses for one reason or another and this is often a circumstance used to justify dishonest selling tricks. Owners with rowdy horses may administer tranquilizers secretly before permitting potential buyers to see their horse or before taking their horse into the auction ring. Pain killers may be given to horses with a limp in their walk to trick people at the auction into thinking that the horse is sound, and a good buy, but no one knows if the meat buyer is going to offer the highest bid in the end or not.

Sport horse owners and/or trainers, especially of race horses that are either too old or injured to perform anymore are known to pump their animals full of every kind of medication, whether prescribed for horses or not, to enhance their performance up to the very end of their careers. While some do not fit this description, many do and often horses are considered money makers so, when they stop bringing in the pay cheques they are worthless to their owners. These are the owners who often do not care where their horses end up and look for the fastest method of disposal for their horses so they have the least possible expenses while the horse isn't "paying for its keep" and often intentionally sell directly to a "meat man" because they are guaranteed to make a small profit. At the same time this option guarantees no one else will benefit from the bloodlines of a particular horse if the original owner is not interested in taking the time to breed it himself.

Unfortunately in many states it was made legislation that it is the owners' responsibility to determine whether the horse they are selling to the slaughterhouse is in sound enough condition to survive the possible several day trip to the meat plant. This is true for pregnant mares as well, it is the owners' (who are the ones making a profit off of the horses going for slaughter) decision to determine whether the mare will give birth before she arrives at the slaughter house or not. Veterinarians across the continent have stated that it is not possible to judge exactly when a mare will give birth, not to mention the fact that often the owners are just out to make a buck when they are selling directly to a slaughterhouse.

The "meat buyers" become the owners of these horses destined for the dinner table just before they are loaded onto the trailer that will deliver them to their final destination, and it is their livelihood to sell horses to slaughterhouses! These facts should pose at least a little skepticism to the validity of their judgments. Following are the only requirements of the USDA for horse transportation to slaughter as stated on their public website (http://www.aphis.usda.gov/vs/nahps/ equine/horse_transport/truckers-brochure/truckers-brochure.html):

> Prior to the commercial transportation of horses to a slaughtering facility, the owner or shipper must:
>
> - Give each horse an opportunity to eat and drink for a period of not less than 6 consecutive hours immediately before loading the animal in the vehicle.
>
> - Apply a USDA backtag to each horse in the shipment with a bar code and a production date. (Backtags are available at recognized slaughtering establishments or from APHIS personnel.)
>
> - Complete and sign an owner/shipper certificate that includes the name, address, and phone number of the shipper and receiver (slaughter plant) and the transporting vehicle's license and registration number.
>
> - Certify that each horse is able to bear weight on all four limbs, is not blind in both eyes, is able to walk unassisted, is not a mare that is likely to foal during the trip, is older than 6 months, and has had access to food, water, and rest for 6 consecutive hours before being loaded into a vehicle.
>
> - Document identifying marks (brands, tattoos, scars, etc.).
>
> - Document breed, color, and sex.
>
> - Document any preexisting condition of the animal prior to shipment to prove the condition did not occur during transport.
>
> Falsification of any certificate or document is a criminal offense and may result in a fine of up to $10,000 or imprisonment for not more than 5 years, or both.

Note that no veterinary advice or approval is even suggested. Note also that there are only three equine slaughterhouses in the United States (two in Texas, Dallas crown Inc. and Beltex Corporation, and one in Illinois, Cavel International which just re-opened in July of 2004) and "meat buyers" may be traveling for several days, through many different states before they arrive at any one of these. There is no requirement for the shippers to provide food, water or rest to the horses during their trip to the slaughterhouse mentioned in the above guide. This is absolutely inhumane and entirely avoidable.

Sadly selling a horse for slaughter is the only option horse owners have that guarantees them a small profit off an unwanted, but not useless horse, and eliminates any disposal efforts or expenses. It needs to be noted that the "meat buyers" are in their business to make a profit, so often that means they have some facility to house any horses they cannot take immediately to the slaughterhouse. This is often due to underweight issues, and in order to make a sustainable income from their line of work, they will make every attempt to fatten up these "unsatisfactory" or, very young, horses. The period of time the horses will spend with the meat buyer depends on its condition at the time they are intended to be shipped to the slaughterhouses. This means that horses who appear to be in good physical condition will go to the slaughterhouses shortly after they are purchased from an auction ring, racetrack, show stable, or simply a backyard owner. These are the ones that are most likely to have traces of one or more medications for various purposes in their bodies, and these are the ones who end up slaughtered first, which makes the risk of not meeting the withdrawal periods of these medications a very real one.

At the slaughterhouse, horses are supposed to be examined by a health inspector (in the United States the inspector is from the United States Department of Agriculture) after they have been slaughtered.

> In the United States, every equine carcass is examined by a USDA inspector. If it does not meet the USDA requirements for quality, the entire carcass winds up in the offal bin, along with intestines and other parts of the anatomy not used for human consumption. This means that such an animal purchased by the plant yields zero return, something no business can afford.[2]

The lack of profit this causes indicates that it doesn't happen often, but it still happens. This is an absolute waste of a life.

The USDA regulations for horses are more strict than they are for other animal species commonly intended for slaughter because the horse meat is exported primarily to Europe and must meet the European Union regulations as well. This means that USDA inspectors force the slaughterhouse workers to throw out entire carcasses as explained above, as well as forcing them to remove and discard

---

2.   Sellnow, "Lined for Slaughter," 27.

any piece of carcass which shows signs of bruising. Before the animals are slaughtered the USDA inspector is supposed to examine each horse and have any horse showing signs of infection, high fever or central nervous system dysfunction removed from the group headed to their deaths. These living, unsatisfactory horses are then "humanely dispatched, but the meat is condemned and must be discarded."[3]

There are no regulations for blood or tissue samples to be taken from *each* of the horses while they are still alive, nor after they have been slaughtered. As stated previously, the horses who appear sound are the ones who are delivered to the slaughterhouses first, and are also the most likely to have had some type of medication administered to them before they left the auction ring, the boarding stable or the racetrack. This is exactly why it is such a dangerous practice for domestic horses to go to slaughter for human consumption.

E-mail correspondence with a woman studying marine biology, also concerned with the issue of horse slaughter and "currently conducting bioassays to determine what, if any, products labeled 'not for use in horses intended for food' are found in commercially processed horse meat," has indicated that the USDA inspections do not seem to always meet the standards. The results of these bioassays from the Texas A&M University are quite scary. The researcher says, "although my data is not in publishable form yet, I can tell you that each of the common de-wormers have been found in quantities above those deemed acceptable by the USDA. In addition, I have found certain tranquilizers and antibiotics above acceptable levels."[4]

The USDA public internet documents show that they do not test horses for some of the most commonly administered medications. In actuality, only a small portion of horse meat intended for human consumption is ever (randomly) tested at all! This is a very real problem, because while cattle and poultry and swine, etc. are often raised with the intension of eventual slaughter for human consumption, in North America (and Australia) horses are not. So, horse owners are not concerned about regularly feeding or injecting prescribed or common medications and pesticides to their animals throughout the period of their ownership, that render the horse unacceptable for human consumption. This is why there needs to be more awareness, world wide, about the process of horse meat reaching the dinner table; it is often tainted with known human carcinogens and is not being adequately tested to ensure its consumers are safe.

---

3.   Sellnow, "Lined for Slaughter," 23.
4.   Sara Black, e-mail message to author, Nov 4, 2004.

Two local government veterinarians Dr. Wannamaker and Dr. Goltz, among the top in their fields, provided a list and description of the most commonly used medications in equine health services for the purpose of this essay. These include anti-inflammatory agents, antibiotics, tranquilizers or sedatives, and de-wormers that are used by professional equine veterinarians regularly. They also provided indications for using these medications and the withdrawal periods required when using the patient for meat. The following is the information supplied by these veterinarians from the New Brunswick Department of Agriculture, Fisheries and Aquaculture:

1. Benamine (medical name: *Flunixin meglumine*)

    Indications: used to alleviate inflammation and pain associated with musculoskeletal disorders and visceral (gut) pain associated with colic

    Withdrawal: ideally should not be given to horses intended for food, but if it occurs, then 14 days withdrawal from the last injection can be used for a meat withdrawal.

2. Bute (medical name: *phenylbutazone*)

    Indications: used to alleviate inflammatory conditions of the horse associated with the musculoskeletal system

    Withdrawal: Should not be used in horses intended for food. A 60 day withdrawal has been suggested for horse meat.

3. Penicillin

    Indications: an antibiotic, used to treat bacterial infections that are sensitive to penicillin

    Withdrawal: 21 days for meat

4. Trimethoprim-sulfa

    Indications: an antibiotic, used to treat bacterial infections that are sensitive to trimethoprim-sulfa

    Withdrawal: 10 days for meat

5. Dormosedan (medical name: *detomidine hydrochloride*)

    Indications: a sedative and analgesic (which means it has some pain relieving properties) used for minor surgeries, some dental procedures, tubing horses via their nose for colic, etc.

    Withdrawal: 7 days for meat

6.   Torbugesic (medical name: *butorphanol*)

Indications: a tranquilizer (sedative) and analgesic, used for relief of pain associated with colic. Can be used in combination with *Xylazine* for tranquilizing effect for minor procedures (ex. Sewing up a cut).

Withdrawal: 7 days for meat

7.   Rompun (medical name: *Xylazine*)

Indications: a sedative and analgesic. Does not have as "strong" a sedative effect as Dormosedan. Sometimes used in combination with *Butorphanol* or alone depending on the horse's temperament.

Withdrawal: 7 days for meat.

8.   Ivermectin

Indications: a de-wormer used for the effective treatment of parasitic infections susceptible to Ivermectin de-wormer. The worms usually killed by Ivermectin are: large strongyles, small strongyles, intestinal thread worms, pin worms, ascarids, hairworms, neck thread worms, stomach worms, at bots.

Withdrawal: 35 days for meat

9.   Strongid (medical name: *pyrantel pamoate*)

Indications: a de-wormer used for the effective treatment of parasitic infections susceptible to Strongid. The worms usually killed are: large strongyles, small strongyles, pin worms, ascarids, and tapeworms.

Withdrawal: 5 days for meat

Consider the fact that de-wormers are supposed to be administered regularly, every two to three months, and the product Bute can be found in just about every stable in Canada and the United States. Note also that these two types of medications have some of the longest withdrawal periods of the above list. With these facts in mind it is obvious that there are many horses, well loved or not, that will end up on the slaughterhouse floor before their withdrawal period is up. As was suggested previously, many horses entering an auction ring have been given common pain killers or anti-inflammatory agents to hide their soreness from potential buyers. The most common medication of choice for pain relief by horse owners and many veterinarians is Bute, which has the longest withdrawal period of all of the above medications.

It was stated earlier that the horses that appear to be in the best physical condition are the ones who are slaughtered first because they will yield the "meat buyer" and the slaughterhouse the highest profits. So if the horses that are purchased from racetracks, show and boarding stables, and auction rings have been given Bute within the last month and a half prior to their sale to the "meat buyer", and they are in good physical condition, chances are they will end up slaughtered, butchered and packaged for export to Europe or Asia for human consumption before their withdrawal period will have ended. The same is true for horses who received a dose of Ivermectin de-wormer in the last three weeks to a month prior to their sale to the "meat buyer". And this is just a few of the common medications for horses, a much longer list was accumulated by request from experienced and everyday horse owners and trainers, for the purpose of this paper.

Some of these medications include anti-inflammatory/analgesics such as DMSO, Ibuprofen, Aspirin, Azium/Dex, Unicort, Boldenon; sedatives like Ace, Barbital; arthritis therapies such as MSM, Chondrotin sulfate, Glucosamine; antibiotics such as sulfa powder, Gentamycin, penicillin; as well as antihistamines, electrolytes, and topical treatments such as Furacin and Hibitane. Each has its own purpose and may or may not have a suggested withdrawal for purposes of using the meat for human consumption. DMSO (Dimethyl Sulfoxide) was one drug in particular that Dr. Goltz also noted that is labeled "do not use on horses intended for slaughter". This is a drug very commonly used on sport horses, especially race horses, as a performance enhancer as well as by medical prescription for injuries. It is restricted to topical use, as it is an external carrying agent directly to the bloodstream. (So, if DMSO was applied to a leg, and then alcohol was put on top of it, the DMSO would carry the alcohol directly to the bloodstream in the leg.) Obviously this has the potential to be a very dangerous drug, and when it is commonly, though not legally, used in sport and race horses as a performance enhancer, when these horses are sold for slaughter they may have traces of this drug in them as well as whatever it carried into their bloodstream!

Horses intended for slaughter for human consumption must be alive when they arrive at the slaughterhouse. Slaughterhouses must kill the horses by way of a stun gun or bullet and are not allowed to employ chemical euthanasia because this would put lethal chemicals into the horses' bodies which would have similarly toxic effects on the human consumers. So why are horses allowed to be slaughtered, packaged, exported and then consumed by humans with a vast number of veterinary chemicals and pesticides in them, many of which are known human carcinogens, without the same level of concern by the officials who determine the health restrictions of animal byproducts?

Sadly there are more horses in the world than there is a demand for as domestic pets or investments, and there are a huge number who are unwanted, and the common excuse is that there is no where else for these unwanted horses to go. This is simply untrue. If the rules and regulations of many horse sports, especially racing, would be altered to allow the animals to have longer careers and decrease the number of injuries, (especially from over working young horses who are not physically developed enough for some stresses) there would be less urgency to get rid of older horses (who, in the racing industry often must "retire" when they are only half their potential, natural age). It would also decrease the urgency placed on producing and racing new, juvenile horses which would help stabilize the horse population, at least in the racing industry. Even if this never happens, with the right amount of time and patience every horse can eventually be sold to a new owner, possibly with a new purpose, and be a perfectly satisfactory pet. The only problem with this solution is that people often do not have the patience, nor do they have the finances to put this much time into a horse in order to sell it, so there needs to be more rescue and rehabilitation facilities to house these unwanted horses temporarily. There is a huge demand for more horse programs for children with handicaps and disabilities, particularly autism. Perhaps the North American governments should look into diverting much of the horse population intended for slaughter that would probably be detrimental to human health, and redirect them to places and programs that can benefit human life.

In order to stabilize the horse population and eliminate the idea that there is no room in the existing North American society for them, we need to discourage unnecessary, unprofessional breeding as well as the understanding that horses are money making machines. Further we need to put an end to the notion that it is perfectly acceptable to dispose of horses when they stop bringing in money and simply buy a new, younger one to replace them. While it is enough for many to oppose horse slaughter simply for ethical reasons, everyone, especially processors and consumers of horse meat, need to take a serious look at the health risks involved with eating once domesticated pets.

Conclusions

"Similarly, when we feel disconnected from the spiritual world, we can turn to horses, just as we turn to the land, to bring this awareness back to our consciousness. If we learn to listen, with patience and reverence, the earth and all its creatures can motivate us to reconnect with our innate wisdom, the part that is most attuned to the rhythms of life. When we become discouraged with our own progress, horses urge us to keep going, to pursue the inner path that connects us with Oneness."[1]

In chatting with my mom today I had some ideas begin to crystallize in my mind about life that I think will be a fitting way to conclude this book. These ideas are no doubt in response to, or reflections of my exposure to, and the processing of events over the past few days in my life and having listened to interviews from Barry Goss and Heather Vale's "Masters of the Secret" series[2]. In any case, they rang very true to my heart as I spoke them today and so, I thought they would be nice to add as an ending to leave you with to contemplate yourself.

First of all, the core idea is that our culture needs to reevaluate its definition and perception of what it means to be selfish. This idea is largely inspired by Randy Gage's suggestion that the world would be a much greater place if everyone were selfish.[3] Quite a controversial idea, I know. Well, it makes a lot of sense the way he describes it. If everyone were selfish—in that they are not necessarily greedy, nasty, or malicious, but if everyone focused on, and made sure that they took care of themselves and their own needs before anything else—if we all made ourselves our first priority, the world would be a better place. And here is why: we

---

1. Adele Von Rust McCormick, Marlena Deborah McCormick, and Thomas McCormick, *Horses and the Mystical Path: the Celtic way of Expanding the Human*, New World Library 2004, 103.
2. Masters of the Secret website access:
   http://www.mastersofthesecret.com/?join=28213
3. I heard this idea from Randy Gage in his interview with Barry Goss and Heather Vale in their "Masters of the Secret" series.

are only in a position to truly, generously and genuinely give of ourselves to any-thing or anyone *after* we are taken care of.

I am learning that we all need to learn, or remember, to love ourselves first. It seems to me that many people, in my culture at least, who are not completely sat-isfied in life are also neglecting themselves. So many of us hold the views that it is evil and immoral to be rich, but noble and good to be poor. But why? Why should we cling to an idea that suffering is good and abundance is bad when ulti-mately the former inspires in us negative emotional and mental states and the lat-ter positive ones? This does not make sense to me.

Why do we cling to limiting beliefs like questioning whether or not we are 'deserving' enough to have pleasure and happiness? Shouldn't we all expect that since pleasure creates in us a positive state that it is not just good for us, but that it also must bring, or activate, pleasure and positive energy to the universe? It just seems silly to me to doubt our own worthiness of greatness, abundance, and plea-sure, and I will attempt to articulate why below.

As I explained earlier, I believe that we are spiritual beings first, just mani-fested in our current physical forms temporarily–for the duration of this life. When we finish this life our soul still exists, just as it did before we were born. I believe that all of our souls are connected and really just components–like puzzle pieces–of a greater whole that is ultimately the Universe. When I refer to we and us here I mean all beings, nonhuman animals, plants, birds–all of us. Essentially, I believe we are all energy; energy is what our souls are and that is what the Uni-verse is, and ultimately these two things are one in the same.

Now that you know a bit about my perspective on this topic I can elaborate on my newest ideas. Basically, it occurs to me that we should all live in abun-dance, joy, and gratitude as often as possible. I believe that it should be our pri-mary goal and innate responsibility to take care of ourselves in this life. I believe it is important to contribute to the greater society and the world, but it should be the ultimate priority of every person on this earth to strive to live the fullest and most joyful life possible. I envision this to mean that each day everyone strives to have as many positive emotions and feelings of genuine gratitude and love that it radiates off of us. And I believe this to be a positive and very important philoso-phy for a couple of reasons.

First, if we are all pieces of the Universe as I believe, then taking care of our-selves and making our lives wonderful is effectively making our piece of the uni-verse one full of joy, gratitude, and positive energy. But second, according to the Law of Attraction–or my understanding of it–just by virtue of being genuinely grateful, we are calling into existence more things to have gratitude for. How wonderful is that? And we all feel it—when someone in a joyful mood enters the room it just naturally brings light and brightens the environment, inspiring and spreading that positive energy wherever they go.

Essentially what this means is that by taking care of ourselves and taking responsibility for making our personal component of the Universe a positive and genuinely grateful one, we are also giving or spreading more of that gratitude and positive energy to the rest of the Universe as well. By taking care of ourselves, being 'selfish,' and focusing on making ourselves truly happy, joyful and grateful, we are giving these same wonderful feelings and intensions as gifts to the rest of the Universe.

If you follow me so far, what I am saying is that by giving to ourselves—finding ways and things to focus ourselves on that make us truly filled with gratitude permits us to not only be happy ourselves, but also to overflow with and just naturally inspire these same feelings in others with the abundance of our own positive attitudes and emotions. But I really believe the trick is in ensuring our own positive state first. If we take responsibility for our own happiness we will naturally and automatically spread this gift to others as we overflow with an abundance of joy. But if we neglect ourselves and then try to give or inspire joy and gratitude in others it won't be nearly as effective, if at all. To truly and honestly give or be generous, we must only give the overflow of our own abundance. For example, if we do not have an abundance of money and we want to be generous, giving is not pleasurable. Tithing should always bring joy, not stinginess, begrudging feelings, guilt or anxiety. If when you give something away and some part of you feels it will be deprived because of this, then it is not true generosity. The positive intension the giver tries to set out is neutralized by the negative feelings it brings to the part of themselves that feels starved or stolen from. So basically, we only have to give, or we only *should* give away the extra, the abundance that we do not feel attached to, so that positive intension of giving stays positive.

Everyone has heard the budgeting rule that we need to pay ourselves first. This is true for money, but also for every other aspect of life. We need to pay ourselves first financially so we create a savings and build wealth for ourselves, *then* we can think about tithing and giving away any extra money we don't feel a need for. The same is true beyond financial saving and giving though. We need to love ourselves before we can really, honestly love anyone else. If we aren't overflowing with love for ourselves, how can we give love away to anyone else? It creates problems in all relationships when people don't take responsibility for loving themselves enough—loving themselves until they are full. When we neglect this, we begin to expect our friends, family, and partners to make us feel loved. This is dangerous because it creates a draining atmosphere and it becomes a need-based relationship. No one likes being on the giving end of a needy relationship because the abundance we share is not appreciated and paid forward, it is expected and hoarded. In order for any relationship to be healthy, each party must be a whole, abundant, and overflowing individual first, before they can contribute to anything positive to a friendship or relationship. This is true for husbands and wives, mothers and daughters, brothers and sisters, etc. It is just the way it is.

So really, from this perspective, in order to even be a good friend, son or daughter, partner or parent, we must be 'selfish.' We must take care of ourselves and take responsibility for our own happiness and gratitude before we can begin to want or try to be a good contributor to anyone else's life or really anything else in life.

When we focus on being grateful and joyful ourselves, we bring happiness to our own lives, make our piece of the Universe more positive, and spread that joy to people we know and complete strangers as we overflow with it. So you see, there is no room in our lives to accept stinginess, anxiety, or doubts of our own worthiness. When we accept and cling to these things not only do we demean ourselves and put ourselves in a negative state, but we also do a great disservice to the rest of the Universe as a whole. The way I see it, not only is it a good idea to do what makes us feel joy and gratitude, it is our responsibility to seek these things out and enjoy them for the highest good of the whole universe. Give it a shot! See how many people you bring a smile to by being in a state of absolute joy and gratitude today!

I hope that these essays have inspired some thought on just what 'God' and the Universe are, what it means to be religious versus spiritual, the relationship between and respective values of human and non human animals, and most importantly, how each of these ideas or concepts is likely to generate a different thought or belief to each individual who contemplates them. While it may be easier to express ourselves if everyone held exactly the same beliefs, it is diversity that acts as a natural safeguard against disaster and devastation for all things in nature.

We are learning now that mono-cropping in agriculture and forestry works great on the short term, but rapidly loses all viability as soil nutrients are depleted and the whole plot of vegetation becomes increasingly vulnerable to pests and diseases. I believe this same concept can be applied to all things, including belief systems–diversity is 'the spice of life' as the saying goes, and when we meet people who disagree and challenge our beliefs we find an opportunity for personal growth. It is in these instances, and through these conversations or debates that we are given a platform to contemplate, evaluate, defend, and perhaps add to or improve on our beliefs by listening to the challenges and different perspectives the other person offers.

Ultimately, I believe the key components in any and all situations are respect and gratitude. In order to truly learn from anyone or any circumstance, we must have respect for those we are dealing with, no matter how different they or their ideas may be to us. Without respect, we cannot legitimately see the individual or their perspective, our view is blurred and we are the ones disadvantaged because of it. And the second part–gratitude, is equally important. Not only must we respect all those around us, but I believe we must also show gratitude for them, and for the opportunity to share with and learn from the experience, environment, and company we encounter. I want to emphasize that my beliefs about respect and gratitude extend beyond other people to include all life–plants, animals, and the natural world as a whole.

Gratitude and greatness share the same root; only when we can live, feeling gratitude for all things, will we begin to see our own true greatness revealed. This is my truth. It is with this goal and lifestyle that we may begin to recognize our personal connection with one another and everything in the Universe and truly move toward Oneness.

Sources for **What If?**:

About.com. "Creation of the Universe". ©2006 About, Inc., A part of The New York Times Company. http://islam.about.com/od/creation/a/creation.htm

Dickinson, Richard; Barth, Karl; and Aquinas, Thomas, "How Do We Know God? (A Radio Conversation between Karl Barth and Thomas Aquinas)" *Journal of Bible and Religion*, Vol. 26, No. 1 (Jan., 1958): 38-43.

Huff, Margaret C., and Wetherilt, Ann K. *Religion: A Search for Meaning*. New York: McGraw-Hill, New York 2005.

Miller, Donald. *Blue Like Jazz*. Nelson Books: 2003.

MSN Encarta. http://encarta.msn.com/ Encyclopedia Article: "Atom". © 2006 Microsoft. http://encarta.msn.com/encyclopedia_761567432/Atom.html

Redfield, James. *The Celestine Prophesy*. New York: Warner Books 1997.

Sources for **Connecting Animal Cruelty with Human Slavery**:

Animals in the History of Western Thought: Part One. From "Animal Rights and Human Obligations", edited by Tom Regan and Peter Singer, 2nd Ed., 1989.

BOSTON ECOFEMINIST ACTION: Founded 2001 http://womensissues.about.com/gi/dynamic/off-site.htm?site=http%3A%2F%2Fwww.geocities.com%2Fbostonecofem%2F

Gelven, Michael. This Side of Evil. Milwaukee, WI, USA: Marquette University Press, 1998. http://site.ebrary.com/lib/unblib/Doc?id=2001907

Roberts, Monty. *The Man Who Listens To Horses*, Vintage Canada, of Random House of Canada Ltd., 1998.

Official Monty Roberts website, http://www.montyroberts.com/

Scanlan, Lawrence. *Wild About Horses: Our Timeless Passion for the Horse*, Random House of Canada Ltd., 1998.

Mott. Maryann. "U.S. Wild Horse Slaughter Legislation Draws Fire." NationalGeographic.com. March 10, 2005. http://news.nationalgeographic.com/ news/2005/03/0310 050310 wildhorses. html (accessed October 6, 2006).

Sources for **Vibrational Medicine & Animal Consciousness**:

Bach, Edward. The Essential Writings of Dr. Edward Bach: The Twelve Healers and Heal Thyself. London: Vermilion, 2005.

Ball, Stefan. The Bach Remedies Workbook: A study Course in the Bach Flower Remedies. London: Vermilion, 2005.

Ball, Stefan. Thorsons Principles of Bach Flower Remedies. London: Thorsons, 1999.

Ball, Stefan and Howard, Judy. *Bach Flower Remedies for Animals*. United Kingdom: Vermilion, 2004.

Fratteroli, Elio. Healing the Soul in the Age of the Brain. Library of America, 2001.

Fulton, Elizabeth and Prasad, Kathleen. Animal Reiki: Using Energy to Heal the Animals in Your Life. Ulysses Press: Berkeley, 2006.
Gotz, Blome M.D. Advanced Bach Flower Therapy: A scientific Aproach to Diagnosis and Treatment. Vermont: Healing Arts Press, 1999.

Hasnas, Rachel. The Essence of Bach Flowers. California: The Crossing Press, 1999.

Howard, Judy Ramsell. The Bach Flower Remedies: Step by Step. United Kingdom: C.W. Daniel Company Limited, 1990.

McCutcheon, Lynn. "Bach Flower Remedies: Time to Stop Smelling the Flowers?" *Skeptical Inquirer* (July/August 1995).

Rand, William Lee. Reiki: The Healing Touch. First and Second Degree Manual. JRT & Hayashi Healing Guide Ed. Vision Publications: Michigan, 2000.

Sabrina, Tamisha. UK Reiki Federation, "The Science Behind Reiki: What Happens in a Treatment?" *Canadian Reiki Association Newsletter*, January 2005.

Weeks, Nora <u>The Medical Discoveries of Edward Bach Physician</u> United Kingdom: Vermillion, 2004.

Website: Bach Shop Direct, "The Remedy Chooser"
http://www.bachshop.co.uk/catalog/index.php/cPath/32

Sources for **Feminist Critiques of Science Contributes to the Debate:**

Birke, Lynda., *Feminism, Animals and Science: The Naming of the Shrew.* Open University Press 1994 Buckingham

De Waal, Frans B.M., "How Animals Do Business" *Scientific American* April 2005 Vol. 292, No.4, pages 73–79.

Hubbard, Ruth., "Have only Men Evolved?" In *Biological Woman—The Convenient Myth: A Collection of Feminist Essays and a Comprehensive Bibliography*, edited by Hubbard, Ruth.; Henifin, Mary Sue.; and Fried, Barbara. Cambridge, MA: Schenkman Pub. Co., 1982.

Rotherton, P.N.M.; Clutton-Brock, T.H.; Gaynor, D.; Griffin, A.S.; Kansky, R.; Manser, M.; and O'Riain, M.J. "Selfish Sentinels in Cooperative Mammals." *Science* 284 (1999): 1640-1644.

Slater, P.J.B., *Essentials of Animal Behavior*. University Press, Cambridge: 1999.

Sources for **Health Risks of Eating Our Pets**:

Animal and Plant Health Inspection Service, United States Department of Agriculture official webite: http://www.aphis.usda.gov

Dr. Goltz, Veterinarian of New Brunswick Department of Agriculture, Fisheries and Aquaculture

Dr. Wannamaker, Veterinarian of New Brunswick Department of Agriculture, Fisheries and Aquaculture

Food Safety and Inspection Service, United States Department of Agriculture "Domestic Residue Data Book" website: http://www.fsis.usda.gov/ophs/redbook1/redbook1.htm

Food Safety and Inspection Service, United States Department of Agriculture. Records of Domestic Residue Monitoring Plans: http://www.fsis.usda.gov/ophs/blue2002/sec4tab.pdf

Just Say Whoa to Horse Slaughter website: http://www.justsaywhoa.org

Kaufman City, Texas website, Horse Slaughter link: http://www.kaufmanzoning.net/horsemeat/Vacca12272003.htm

Sara Black, Texas A&M University's Benthic Lab, Galveston, TX 77551

Sellnow, Les. *Lined for Slaughter.* The Horse: Your Guide to Equine Health Care Magazine, December Issue: 1999.

Society for Animal Protective Legislation Frequently Asked Questions website: http://www.saplonline.org/Legislation/ahspa/faq.htm

978-0-595-44353-6
0-595-44353-2

www.ingramcontent.com/pod-product-compliance
Lightning Source LLC
Chambersburg PA
CBHW051428280526
45785CB00003B/1203